LEARN TO RIDE
USING
SPORTS PSYCHOLOGY

A TRAINING AID FOR RIDERS AND INSTRUCTORS

PETRA AND WOLFGANG HÖLZEL

Translated by Christina Belton

Trafalgar Square Publishing

First published in the United States of America in 1996 by
Trafalgar Square Publishing
North Pomfret
Vermont 05053

**Printed and bound in Great Britain by
WBC Book Manufacturers Ltd, Bridgend**

English Language Edition © The Kenilworth Press Ltd 1996

First published in Germany under the title *Mentales Training für Reiter*, by
Franckh-Kosmos Verlags-GmbH & Co., Stuttgart, in 1995
© Franckh-Kosmos Verlags-GmbH & Co., Stuttgart, 1995

English language edition published simultaneously in Great Britain by
The Kenilworth Press Ltd and in the United States of America by
Trafalgar Square Publishing in 1996.

Library of Congress Catalog Card Number: 96-60231

ISBN 1-57076-063-2

Disclaimer of Liability
The Authors and Publisher shall have neither liability nor responsibility
to any person or entity with respect to any loss or damage caused or alleged
to be caused directly or indirectly by the information contained in this book.
While the book is as accurate as the Authors can make it, there may be
errors, omissions, and inaccuracies.

Typeset in 10/13 Palatino
Typesetting and layout by Kenilworth Press

Publisher's Note
This book is a translation from the German *Mentales Training für Reiter* and includes a
few photos of German riders without hard hats. **It is the publisher's view that for
safety's sake an appropriate hard hat should always be worn when riding.**

CONTENTS

INTRODUCTION

Learn to Ride Using Sports Psychology is not just another book about learning to ride. Instead it offers a new approach using modern training techniques that already have a long record of success in other sports. Whilst the **classical principles of riding** remain unaltered, what is different here is the **method of teaching and learning them.** In this book we have translated this method into a practical system, relating it to the individual phases of rider training.

The book is primarily **aimed at the beginner** – taking him from his first encounter with horses up to early dressage and jumping competitions. It is also **aimed at his instructor.** It is pitched at a fairly basic level because it has been shown that the benefits of psychological training are by no means restricted to 'high-flyers' striving for extraordinary achievements. In fact, **psychological training can benefit the everyday rider, and moreover can be learned by anyone.** It enables the beginner to make rapid, trouble-free progress, which is essential if he is to continue to enjoy his sport and his training.

Successful competitors have been using this method, either consciously or purely instinctively, from time immemorial. What is new is the realisation that anyone can learn, practise and use it. Instead of leaving the outcome of your training to chance, you will be able to obtain consistently good results which can be reproduced and repeated. It is therefore particularly important that beginners learn using the psychological approach, since it lays the foundation for future progress and results. The rider who has learned by this method will also experience far fewer problems later on when he encounters the more difficult exercises.

The fact that this book is aimed at the beginner does not mean that he will be the only one to benefit from it. Far from it. The exercises described are examples, and can easily be adapted to **all levels of horsemanship,** and indeed to life outside the realms of sport.

We, the authors, learned to ride by

traditional methods, and later instructed in the same way. We sometimes encountered difficulties and had our questions and doubts, yet over the course of decades we found no satisfactory solution – until, that is, we came across this fascinating training system. Let us explain briefly the events which led up to this discovery.

At a relatively early point in our careers, we became unhappy with loud, authoritarian commands, and with the lack of satisfactory answers to questions about the causes of success or failure. Even today, some riding schools still display a sign which says "Riding is only learned by riding!" This means that, as a means of learning something, you are being called upon to do the very thing which you want to learn – which of course you do not yet know. This is no help when it comes to knowing **how** to do it!

The actual method of learning often consists of 'practice, practice and more practice'. What this really means is that you go on and on until you grind to a halt. Instead of practice making perfect, things simply go from bad to worse, and the result is failure for horse and rider.

In Germany this is what we call the 'army loaf method', after a story told to us by an ex-cavalryman who had very skilfully adapted military methods to the training of civilian riders. The story goes that some new recruits arrived at the barracks, and among them was a hulk of a man with a reputation for being able to polish off an entire army loaf at one sitting. The sergeant told his superior, who would not believe it, and between them they made a bet. The next morning they were lying in wait

with one of the mighty loaves, ready to test the story. The recruit failed to get past the second mouthful. The sergeant was bewildered: "I don't believe it," he said, "only a minute ago we practised it three times, and everything was fine!"

The search for an effective method of learning and teaching has taken us decades. Attempts to apply developments in educational theory, psychology and sports science to instruction at the German national riding centre, the 'Deutsche Reitschule', brought about some progress, but not enough to satisfy us. Corrections were either not put into practice, or the effects were not lasting. Even dressage clinics on a one-to-one basis and with video replay did not produce the desired results. Most noticeable of all, however, was the fact that in competitions or examinations, all the good results so painstakingly obtained beforehand seemed to evaporate. Old patterns of behaviour, and with them all the old faults, reappeared unchanged.

In the case of follow-up courses (preparatory courses for professional instructor examinations and 'improver' courses for professionals and amateurs), not only had the participants not improved, but they had usually deteriorated. Hence the instruction they had received did not seem to have a lasting effect. In particular, in most cases there was a distinct and unmistakable drop in performance in an examination situation.

The same problems also arose when training private students abroad (Australia and Canada): you could not rely on the instruction being effective in the long term. After a long break (six months or more), nothing or hardly anything remained of what had been learned; progress from one session to the next did not seem possible.

In examination or competition situations, even when breaks in training were much shorter, the student seemed to have forgotten everything which had been explained and practised at length, even the warm-up technique.

We still sought answers to the following questions:

- How, for the least possible outlay in terms of effort, can riders form new patterns of behaviour which can be relied upon to hold out under stress (in examinations and competitions)?

- How can any rider effectively turn defective patterns of behaviour into correct ones?

- How can riders ensure that sequences of movements, such as a dressage test, course of show-jumps, or cross-country round, which are correctly done during practice, are so well established that they can be reliably reproduced even in the most stressful situation (even up to world championship or Olympic level)?

- How can the student be made more and more self-sufficient in the assessment of his performance?

- How can he continue to make progress when he is working alone afterwards, and hence having to monitor himself?

- How can the above improvements be attained through a reasonable

number of exercises, that is, without making excessive demands, especially on the horse?

If you ask questions for long enough, you will eventually receive an answer. In our case it was due to a chance piece of information which we followed up. In 1987 we saw a television interview with skier Frank Wörndl, whom we had never heard of, and who had just unexpectedly become the world champion in downhill. He explained that he owed thanks for his success in particular to a professor of sports psychology, Herr Eberspächer, from Heidelberg, and his system of psychological training. Professor Eberspächer had for the first time enabled Wörndl to influence his inner self to best effect, and to realise and exploit to the full his sporting potential. Not a sports professional or a ski instructor but a professor of psychology! We found this so unusual and exciting that it aroused our curiosity, and we immediately looked him up in the telephone directory, and called Heidelberg. We were given an appointment for an interview a few days later, along with an invitation to stay overnight and visit the 'Sportinstitut'. When we met Professor Eberspächer we soon found ourselves engaged in an extremely interesting conversation about new ways of handling sports training and sporting performance and directing it towards optimum results. The method involved the use of consciously enacted psychological processes. Through this system of mental training he had successfully trained sportsmen from almost every discipline (boxers, cyclists, motorcyclists, archers and swimmers, as well as skiers), and had even convinced the official national coaches. This seemed to be the very learning and teaching method for which we had searched for so long. It was during this conversation that the idea for this book was conceived.

We were fascinated and filled with enthusiasm, and determined to study this method in as much detail as possible, and above all to try applying it to equestrianism. In the meantime we read numerous books by English and American authors who had obtained considerable success in other sports with this method. Our aim was to apply their knowledge to the process of learning to ride. We set about achieving this through seminars with riding instructors, through the mutual exchange of experiences, and above all

through our own work instructing competition riders, 'normal users', youngsters and adults, both in individual and class lessons. The results were astonishing, and above all they could be reproduced and repeated, and were consistent even in competition and examination situations.

We hope that you also will benefit from our experiences and will be fascinated by this method, which will also yield benefits in other areas of life. Above all, though, it will enable you to have more consistently successful experiences with your equine partner in your chosen sport, and so also to obtain greater fulfilment and enjoyment.

Petra Hölzel
Wolfgang Hölzel

1

PSYCHOLOGICAL TRAINING

1.1 WHAT IS PSYCHOLOGICAL TRAINING?

Psychological training is a method of learning and teaching which enables us to greatly influence and improve physical performance through mental processes, using the mind and feelings. In recent years this method has achieved astonishing results in a wide range of sports.

For many sports journalists, the word 'psychological' has become indispensable. For example, we hear that a tennis player is not 'psyched up', that a sprinter is 'psychologically burned out', or that a skier needs to work especially on his psychological, or mental, preparation. In other words, it is not physical fitness alone, but attitude, powers of concentration, self-confidence and the will to win, which provide the winning 'edge'.

Successful sportsmen have always made use of psychological training, if only instinctively. The tennis player

who reacts to a successful shot by raising a clenched fist is giving himself the incentive to do it again. When, after an unsuccessful stroke, he makes a corrected version in the air without the ball, he is consciously or unconsciously making use of psychological training methods.

The intense concentration of sprinters, high-jumpers, long-jumpers, swimmers and ice-skaters before the start, is clearly written on their faces. But this is not something which has emerged with the advent of psychological training. When a certain successful boxer proclaimed himself 'the greatest', as a means not only of intimidating his opponent, but of inciting himself to peak performance, this was an instinctive rather than a considered, trained reaction.

In equestrianism it has been apparent for decades that the really successful riders, waiting to enter the jumping arena, sit immersed in thought, going over the course yet again in their mind, either pointing at the jumps

Before entering the arena, many riders like to cut themselves off completely from their surroundings and mentally rehearse the test or course.

because success can also take the form of an enhanced partnership with the horse, resulting in greater enjoyment. Psychological training is, beyond doubt, a key to success for the competition sportsman, but it is also a valuable asset for every rider.

> **IMPORTANT** Psychological training is a key to success and can be systematically learned by amateur and pleasure riders.

Through training your **body awareness**, or **feel**, for instance, you experience the horse's movements more consciously and more intensely. You learn to 'tune in' to yourself and your horse, to be aware of your movements and to refine your aids more and more. Because you have learned to use your mind to control your feel and your actions, you will make progress which you will find enjoyable in itself, so that you will not feel it essential to have your achievements acknowledged in the competition arena.

individually, or with closed eyes. Many of the great dressage riders have been seen to sit for long periods with their eyes closed before entering the arena, while others, before warming up, withdraw to a quiet corner, their car or the trailer, and become totally lost to the outside world.

Psychological training is not, then, intrinsically new. It was already being used instinctively by successful performers. What is new is the discovery that it can be learned systematically, and hence that it is accessible to anyone who is prepared to submit to the learning process. It is a useful tool for anyone, even the amateur, the person who rides in his spare time as a hobby and who is not primarily concerned with success – or perhaps we should say, with success which can be measured externally,

Psychological training, like any form of training, will only be effective if you try it out and practise it intensively enough and for a long enough period. If you do not start it until just before a test or competition, you can hardly expect it to yield dramatic results.

Applied over a long period, it will bring you great benefits in learning, practising and taking part in competitions: you will develop the ability to visualise sequences of images in your mind, and to run through this 'inner film' as often as and whenever you like. This is called **visualisation** or

Psychological training can benefit all riders, whatever their chosen discipline.

mental rehearsal. You do not have to rely on having to try out and practise everything over and over again on the horse. While you are doing these exercises in your head, your horse is standing peacefully in his stable, and is spared all the unnecessary physical or mental stress!

> **TELL YOURSELF** I can practise any time, anywhere, and as often as I want, without overtaxing my horse.

As a result of training aimed specifically at improving your **powers of concentration**, you will be able to shut yourself off from distractions and focus your energy and skill on the task in hand.

A **positive attitude** helps you to put mistakes behind you and avoid nervousness. You know full well that you are able to do certain things, and that you should manage to do them even in different circumstances (in competition arenas all over the world!). You know that you can – quite realistically – believe in yourself. You do not **have** to win at all costs, but you will get the best out of yourself and your horse.

If your attitude is right you will not feel the need to keep sneaking a look at everyone else, or watching nervously how they ride. You will ride according to your own plan (which has been worked out with your instructor), and judge yourself by the standards you have achieved through psychological training. You will see that it is to your advantage to stick to your plan. So do not allow yourself to be put off, or to be talked out of it by outsiders, or indeed by your opponents.

Once you are convinced that the road you have chosen is the right one, outward signs of success will follow.

method has been applied for the first time to the basics of horsemanship, and set out in a concrete form with clear examples. There is no change in the classical content of the teaching, but the methods of teaching and learning it are new.

1.2 THE SIX MOST IMPORTANT SKILLS FOR CONTROLLING THE MIND

1. Controlled stimulation (tension and relaxation)

• You can alter your own – physical and mental – level of stimulation. Draw up a scale of stimulation ranging from zero (total passivity as in a deep, dreamless sleep) to the highest level of stimulation (as in a state of panic).

• You can learn to control your level of stimulation so that it corresponds exactly with your wishes. You must discover the ratio of 'acceleration', and so activity, to 'braking' or relaxation, which is the most advantageous to your personal performance.

• If, for example, you tend to get so worked up before and during a competition that it 'paralyses' your performance, you can learn to relax by doing special relaxation exercises. If you are this type of person, there should be no danger of you going to the other extreme and lapsing into passivity!

• If you are more inclined to the 'couldn't care less' attitude, you must work yourself up, arouse your 'fighting

You can run through a 'film' of the movements in your head, whenever, wherever and as often as you like.

Through psychological training you can improve your performance. Through it you can learn new movements more easily and effectively than by previous methods. It will certainly enable you to obtain more enjoyment from your sport.

It also allows the instructor to correct faults more easily than if he were using traditional teaching methods; moreover he can be more effective and successful when teaching something new. This will make his job more interesting and productive.

Furthermore, the horse is spared a lot of the tedium and unnecessary torment which can be caused by incorrect, inadequate or simply bad instruction, and by a dissatisfied, frustrated rider.

In this book the psychological

spirit'. You will also find this useful if you are feeling tired and dejected after a sleepless night, or when you have lost your 'edge' through having to wait longer than expected at the start. Too 'laid back' or relaxed an attitude can detract from your keenness: a certain adrenalin 'buzz' is necessary for a competition.

• It is up to you to decide what is your optimum level of stimulation. Of course, your trainer will help you to discover the right point on the scale, and you should discuss the matter in depth with him or her.

As well as certain exercises which are described later, there are some effective ways of regulating your level of stimulation:

a) Your behaviour

To relax, move around slowly or not at all. Breathe deeply and breathe out calmly (see below).

To increase your level of stimulation, move quickly and energetically. Contract your muscles strongly and deliberately, and breathe in consciously.

b) Your environment

To relax, seek out a quiet place with no distractions, listen to peaceful music (perhaps on a walkman or car radio).

To increase your level of stimulation, choose a busy, noisy, exciting environment full of distractions, and loud, rousing music.

c) Your frame of mind

To relax, tune yourself to 'calm' mode; conjure up a pleasant feeling of well-

being ("I feel really good").

To increase your level of stimulation, you need to challenge yourself: put yourself under pressure, be assertive ("Yes!", "I'll show them!", "I want to do it **now**!").

Relaxation is essential to the functioning of your physical and mental faculties. It is a basic criterion, but not an end in itself.

• The ability to relax can be beneficial when in difficult, unfamiliar or stressful situations, and in competitions. However, although being very relaxed, i.e. 'laid back', can improve performance, it is not conducive to peak performance. For the latter, you must draw on your last reserves, and pull out all the stops, and that in a competition situation.

• However (fortunately for the horse!), peak performance is not called for every day. Hence it is for you to judge (which you will learn to do) what degree of 'acceleration' or 'braking' is right for you personally, for your

To relax, seek out a quiet place, free from distractions.

expectations, for what is required and for the overall situation in question.

TELL YOURSELF I can control my level of stimulation.

2. Body awareness and 'feel'

It is because you communicate with the horse through your body, via the aids, that **precise awareness of your body ('feel')**, and conscious control of it are so important in horsemanship.

• You can learn to tune in to each part of the body individually, and to use this ability consciously and in a controlled manner in your riding. This will also enable you to experience and control the horse's movements and reactions much more sensitively.

• You can learn to improve your awareness of your own body, and at the same time your 'feel' for the movement processes and sequences which you and the horse perform together. You will quickly realise when you try out some of the exercises described below that conscious awareness of your body is not the foregone conclusion that it may have seemed at first.

• You will overcome the problems more easily if you understand that 'feel', or body awareness, is the basis of body control, which is the most important tool or 'instrument' in your sport.

INSTRUCTOR'S TIP

Tell yourself: I can obtain results more easily and effectively by training the student's body awareness or 'feel'.

3. Mental rehearsal (visualisation/mental imaging)

You need to learn the skill of picturing the movements in your mind as exactly as when you were riding them. Nerves, muscles, ligaments and tendons react in the same way as during the real thing, though more subtly. What is extraordinary is that afterwards, when you are back in the saddle, your reactions will be exactly as you pictured them mentally!

• So ride an exercise in your mind, including every detail in your mental visualisation. For example, run through a movement such as leg-yield, or through a dressage test or course of jumps, and express what you are doing in words, aloud. This enables you to exercise a high level of self-criticism,

You can ride an exercise in your mind, including every detail.

and also puts your instructor in the best possible position to monitor you.

• You can learn to experience a particularly well-performed exercise all over again in your imagination (with your eyes open or closed, depending on which works best for you), and then to go on to perform it even better.

• When you are riding, a shortened formula, based on a description of the correctly performed movement, will help you to repeat it exactly as before. Cutting down the words to the essentials is helpful because full sentences and descriptions of the movement always take longer than the movement itself. So you use 'prompts' or 'cues' to reduce the description to the actual duration of the movement. The script must not be longer than the 'film' which is playing in your mind!

• With training, you will be able to develop your ability to recreate in your mind all the specific details and feelings of a particular riding experience. This will enable you to 'replay' afterwards and at any time in the future

everything which you do in practice, just as if you were actually riding it again. You can also highlight any points you think require special emphasis.

> **TO SUM UP**   Tell yourself: What you see (i.e. visualise) is what you get!

4. Concentration

It is perfectly possibly to learn to focus your concentration absolutely, and in any given situation, and not to let yourself succumb to any distractions. This is another skill which is developed by training. Start by trying to shut out, just for a short period (approximately the duration of one exercise), all outside influences and all your personal problems.

• Focus all your attention and all your energies on this single task, and do not allow yourself to be side-tracked. With practice, you will learn to concentrate better and better, for longer periods, for the duration of several different exercises, and eventually for a whole

If an exercise goes wrong keep going, and focus all your concentration on the next one.

Don't think about a fence further on in the course – deal with it when you get there.

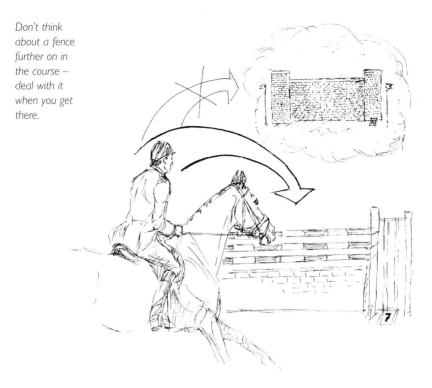

You need to learn to concentrate completely in any situation, and be able to shut out distractions.

dressage test or course of jumps. You should also practise 'putting mistakes behind you'. After a failed exercise, carry on, forget about it, and

concentrate as hard as you can on the lesson ahead.

• Neither must you dwell on the subsequent lesson, or the lesson after that, or some fence further on in the course which may be giving you cause for concern. You must deal with it when it comes up, and not before.

IMPORTANT Tell yourself: By shutting out the past and the future, I am learning to concentrate all my faculties on what matters, i.e. on what lies immediately ahead.

5. Positive attitude (self-confidence)

• Learn to think positively and to develop a confident attitude. Spell out to yourself what you **can** do, and be discreetly proud of it. In this way you

Remind yourself of your achievements.

will sooner come to believe yourself capable of the things which you are (as yet) unable to do. However, the goals you set yourself must be sensible and realistic; they must be attainable.

• Set out what you want to achieve. Here again, think positive. Never tell yourself what you must not do, only what you must do; do not think about the wrong way to do it, only the right way.

• Many people find it difficult to experience positive self-confidence. Perhaps you have been brought up to believe that modesty is a virtue, and that you should never 'blow your own trumpet'. Certainly you should not go around bragging. However, if you want to achieve something, you must drum it into yourself that it is not possible without self-confidence.

• You may be the sort of person who takes every opportunity to criticise yourself and dwell on your weaknesses

– after all, you know your faults better than anyone else does. However, you must force yourself to see your good side.

REMINDER Simply keep telling yourself what you **can** do, that is, what you are good at.

Remind yourself of your achievements (even small things count!), and you will find that this makes it easier to go on to achieve more.

• If you only tell yourself what you cannot do, you are giving yourself no chance to improve. You are thinking only of failure, thus shutting out all thoughts of what would be better or good. You are making it impossible to improve, because you are not entertaining the idea as a possibility, and you are not preparing yourself for it.

IMPORTANT Keep on at yourself: I will tell myself what I **can** do, and what I intend to learn. I will not tell myself what I **cannot** do.

• Self-confidence has nothing to do with having an exaggerated opinion of yourself. Provided you are not one of those people who think they can do anything, regardless of whether they can or not, then you won't run the risk of overestimating yourself. You run a far greater risk of not getting the best out of yourself. You are not a 'big head' or a 'big mouth': you would simply like to achieve something, to 'get somewhere', and to have something to be proud of. The frame of

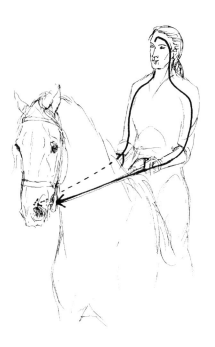

Say to yourself: "I am now taking with both hands an even, steady contact with the horse's mouth."

mind you need to adopt in order to do this can be learned and practised.

6. 'Self talk'

If a skill cannot be translated into words, it cannot it be changed, and so consolidated and improved. Not until it is expressed in words does your action become conscious and tangible. If, in riding, you want to learn, consolidate or change something, you must be in a position to put it into words.

TAKE NOTE By talking things through with yourself, you can reinforce or change your behaviour, or indeed influence it negatively.

• You can make positive affirmations: *I can do it!*

• You can regulate your state of mind: *Stay calm! Keep your cool!*

• Or you can control your actions, and tell yourself what you are supposed to be doing: *I am now taking with both hands an even, steady contact with the horse's mouth.*

• The 'self talk' becomes negative in effect when you tell yourself: *I'll never be able to do it!*

• You can engage in this 'self talk' whilst you are actually riding, but also before and afterwards. If you are trying to confirm or consolidate your actions, keep saying the same thing.

• Your instructor can contribute to your 'self talk' making positive or negative inputs as required. This is a very effective way for him to influence your riding.

• By talking to yourself you can give yourself encouragement, keep your spirits up, and boost your self-confidence: *Come on, you're good enough, you can do it!*

• By talking to yourself you can have a calming influence: *Keep calm, there's no problem, you **can** do it!*

• You can encourage yourself to relax by briefly closing your eyes and saying: *Now breathe out slowly and fully!*

• You can spur yourself on to higher achievements: *This is it! We'll show them!*

• By talking to yourself you can recall and consolidate previous experiences: *Feel just as you did when you won!* or: *Feel the transition from trot to halt exactly as you did yesterday, when it went so well.*

• Reciting key words from your 'self talk' will aid your concentration. For example, when riding a corner: *Flexion, bend, lighter, straighten.*

• You can help yourself to put negative thoughts aside: *This is not the time or the place. Not now, afterwards, when you've finished riding!*

• Engaged in your 'self talk' you will be sealed off from outside influences: you talk to yourself only and shut out other people and your surroundings. Speech is more precise, more conscious and more expressive than inarticulate thoughts or feelings. It makes you concentrate on the essential points.

• 'Self talk' is an excellent way of using all aspects of psychological training more effectively, i.e. of developing relaxation, feel, mental imaging, concentration and self-confidence.

TELL YOURSELF Talking to myself makes it easier to transform my mental skills into actions.

• It is important that your 'self talk' can be heard by your instructor when having a lesson. Ask him to allow you to say out loud what you are trying to do, are doing, or have just done. When you are riding without your instructor, you should also 'think out loud' to start with, so as to learn and reinforce the skill of 'self talk'.

INSTRUCTOR'S TIP

Tell yourself: 'Self talk' is an invaluable tool which I shall resolve to use in my teaching.

• When you are not riding alone, you should recite your 'self talk' in your

Tell yourself: "I **can** *do it!."*

head, rather than aloud. This is definitely the case in tests and competitions! Moreover, you will notice that, as a result of proper training, you become better able to recite your 'self talk' in your head, and so to use this skill in any situation.

1.3 EXERCISES WHICH CAN BE DONE WITHOUT A HORSE

General
All six skills can be practised and improved without a horse: for example at home, while waiting for the bus or train, standing in line at the supermarket, or in the doctor's waiting room.

• Begin with relatively easy exercises which do not demand too much effort and gradually increase the level of difficulty.

• Be aware that many people find even the easier exercises difficult. If they persevere, these people often obtain better results in the long run than those who find everything easy to start with.

• Above all, to make the exercises easier for yourself, begin by creating a pleasant atmosphere, starting with your surroundings. For example, find a quiet room, with no-one else in it. Later you can gradually make conditions more testing, until you are finally able to do the exercise even amidst a milling crowd of people and animals, with the din of music and

You can practise and improve all six skills without being on a horse.

If you are intending to ride a course of jumps, you should be able to run through it fully and precisely in your mind.

loud speakers in the background (that is, in competition conditions).

• It is better to do short exercises as often as possible than long exercises with long intervals between them.

• If you are having problems with an exercise, go back to an easier one. But do have a go at solving the problem first.

• Before you ride a test or course, you should be able to ride it through fully and precisely in your imagination.

• Talk yourself through your visualisation. Do this either in your head or – if you are alone – out loud. Say in a shortened form everything that you intend to do. This will also help you to concentrate for the whole duration of the exercise.

Eventually you will be able to concentrate and run through your mental rehearsal in unfavourable conditions.

• Learn to keep an eye on the clock! The time you spend going through the exercise in your mind should correspond to the amount of time available for riding it. For example, if the time allocated for a dressage test is six minutes, then try to keep to the mental rehearsal to six minutes.

• Particularly when training for a competition, the trainer or instructor should listen to your 'self talk' and correct anything that is wrong. This technique also makes it easier to learn new exercises and to cure faults.

• These exercises work best if you convince yourself that they are helpful and enjoyable.

MAKE UP YOUR MIND   Tell yourself: I will ask my instructor to take part in and help me with my own 'customised' 'self talk'.

• The skills which you acquire through these exercises can be put to use in other areas – their benefits are not restricted to riding.

Keep an eye on the time as you work through the test in your mind.

1. Relaxation and tension (regulating the level of activation or stimulation)

A certain degree of stimulation and excitement, leading to the release of adrenalin into the bloodstream, is a necessity: without it you cannot achieve peak performance in special situations such as tests and competitions. However, if the stimulation becomes too great, you become 'up tight', and the typical symptoms of over-stimulation or tension begin to appear – typically, sweating under the arms, shallow, rapid breathing, and a pounding heart. This sort of tension is detrimental to performance and leads to impaired and incorrect reactions. In this situation you need effective relaxation exercises that you can depend on.

a) Relaxation (reducing tension)

Even people with no prior experience quickly obtain tangible results with these relaxation exercises. Experiment to find out which exercises suit you best. Use combinations of different exercises, and gradually try to arrive at a satisfactory result using less and less effort.

The 'shoulder-breathing' exercise

The 'shoulder-breathing' procedure described below has been found to be an excellent relaxation exercise. It has proved to be very effective and helpful in the most stressful situations, such as world championships and the Olympic Games. However – and this applies equally to the other exercises – it will only be successful if it is practised intensively and over a long period.

And it is not only in the competition arena that it is beneficial: relaxation exercises are just as helpful in day-to-day riding, when you are nervous or tense, when your confidence is at a low

Shoulder-breathing exercise. Draw both your shoulders right up, breathing in deeply as you do so, then hold your breath for 6-7 seconds, breathe out slowly, allowing your shoulders to sink down again.

ebb, or when you become discouraged and feel like giving up.

Try out the following steps:

• Draw up both shoulders towards your ears – and higher still!

• Allow them to sink slowly back down.

• Now draw up your shoulders again, right up to your ears, while breathing in slowly, and hold your breath and position for six to seven seconds.

• Count: one Mississippi, two Mississippi, three Mississippi, four Mississippi, five Mississippi, six Mississippi – while breathing out slowly and at the same time letting your shoulders sink slowly down again.

• After only a few repetitions, you will feel the tension in your muscles ease, and you will experience a feeling of well-being. The exercise does not take long, and you can do it virtually anywhere, in a sitting or standing position. After a while you will be able to put its relaxing, stress-relieving effect to good use in difficult situations such as tests and competitions. It will also enable you to remain calm and objective when you are angry, say, because your boss has 'blown up' at you unfairly!

• As soon as you are able to eliminate the negative effects of tension even in stressful situations, you can begin to shorten the exercise. At the first sign of 'negative' tension, breathe out consciously and fully. You will soon find that this alone has a noticeably beneficial effect. Eventually, you will be able to induce relaxation simply by thinking about breathing out.

Relaxing the face
The most sensitive part of the face is the mouth, so this is the centre point of the exercise. Allow your lower lip, together with your eyelids, to drop.

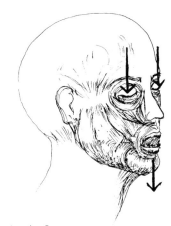

Relaxing the face.

Alternatively, with your mouth slightly open, put your tongue on your upper lip. The 'shoulder-breathing' exercise and the facial exercises have the advantage that you can practise them virtually anywhere when no-one is looking, even in public.

• In stressful and difficult situations of all kinds, not just when you are on the horse, take the opportunity to practise using these relaxation exercises to overcome negative tension and over-reactions.

• Also try the relaxation techniques mentioned earlier: keep still or make slow movements, seek out tranquil surroundings, listen to calm music, or simply tell yourself: "I feel good, I feel well". See which works best for you.

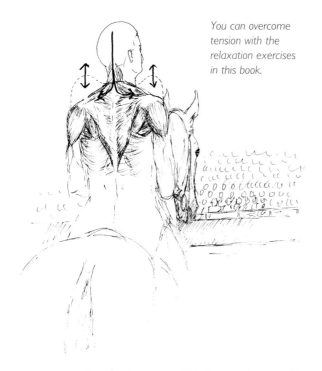

You can overcome tension with the relaxation exercises in this book.

I will give my best! I'll show them! I feel fit and ready for anything!"

• Try tensing your arm and clenching your fist a few times, moving quickly and energetically, increasing stimulation through concentration exercises (see below), seeking out a stimulating environment, and listening to music which stimulates and excites you.

• Exercises to increase stimulation and drive are certainly less necessary for most people than exercises to reduce tension. However, sometimes in life, and in some situations, you will find them very useful.

• Discover which exercises and which conditions best serve to 'activate' you.

KEY POINT Tell yourself: Even in the most stressful and anxious situations, I can overcome tensions and 'blocks' by doing relaxation exercises.

b) Increasing stimulation ('pumping up')

You can also use breathing and facial exercises to stimulate and goad yourself for the fray when you are feeling tired and listless.

• Press your tongue hard against the roof of your mouth for about eight to ten seconds.

• You can also invoke a mood from the past, for example the feeling of triumph you experienced at a competition you won or in which you were well placed.

• Alternatively, talk to yourself: "Now

Think of the feeling of success you experienced, for example, when you won a competition.

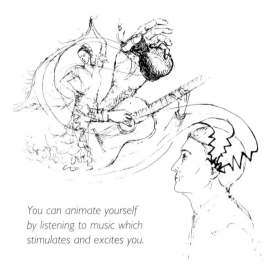

You can animate yourself by listening to music which stimulates and excites you.

2. Body awareness, or 'feel'

• Begin by concentrating on ('feeling') different parts of the body, trying to sense an awareness of, for example, every finger individually, first on your right hand, then on your left, or each of your toes, individually and one at a time. At first, most people need to move the part of the body concerned in order to feel it, and this is normal. It takes a certain amount of practice to tune into the part immediately, without moving it.

Begin by concentrating on the 'feel' of individual parts of the body, for example each finger of first your right hand, then your left.

• Develop this skill by applying it to larger areas of muscle, for example, shoulders, upper arms, forearms, thighs and lower legs. You also need to practise 'feeling' these parts during intensive exercise.

• Using this technique, gradually 'feel' your way down your whole body, from top to bottom. Include the joints too, such as neck, hips, wrists and ankles. Pay special attention to feeling the centre of movement, the hips.

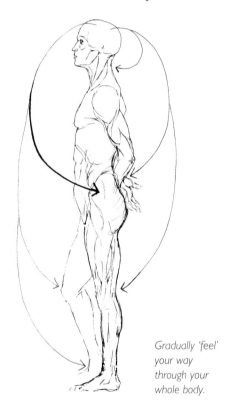

Gradually 'feel' your way through your whole body.

• Try this out at first without the horse, either in a sitting position, lying down or standing up. Then try the same thing in the saddle, at the halt, and when walking at the beginning of a lesson or during breaks.

• Also try to feel the active parts of your body during automatic sequences of everyday movements such as walking, standing up, and climbing stairs.

Try to 'feel' the parts of your body which are active in automatic sequences of movements, such as climbing stairs.

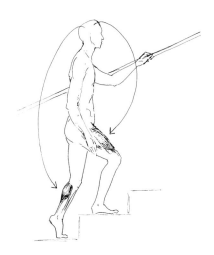

TELL YOURSELF By improving my body awareness, I am creating the best possible conditions for learning new movements and correcting old ones.

3. Mental rehearsal or visualisation

Preparatory exercises
• Begin by finding a quiet place and picturing simple images in your mind: for example a picture of a certain house, a lake or a river.

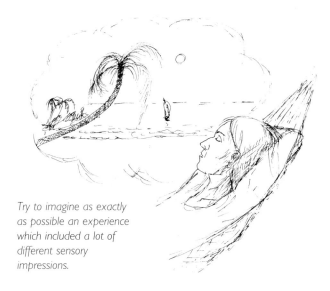

Try to imagine as exactly as possible an experience which included a lot of different sensory impressions.

• Then try to imagine, as precisely as possible, a scene containing many different sensory impressions. Close your eyes and picture something like this: you are lying on a beach; you can see the sea in a certain colour; you can smell the salty sea air; you can feel your body, relaxed in the pleasant warmth of the sun; you can feel the sand underneath you, and hear the waves.

• Discover which of the sensory impressions is the strongest. For example, if it is the visual impression – the colour of the sea – which is the most intense, then you know that visual perception will also later provide the most lasting basis for your images of movements. So, for you, the best and most vivid way of recalling a sequence of movements will be through the visual impressions associated with it. However, if the sound of the waves is the most lasting impression, then you will learn most effectively through 'acoustics', by remembering things which you hear. If this is the case, you will recall the sequence of movements through acoustic impressions. In most people, though, the sensory perceptions are about equal in strength. If you belong to this group, select the one which you are able to recall most easily.

IN THE BEGINNING Finish your exercise as soon as the images become weaker. Do not force yourself to see the picture more clearly, to smell the air more keenly etc. With time and practice, this will come spontaneously. End the exercise by taking a deep breath and opening your eyes.

Exercises in visualisation

• Picture in your mind familiar sequences of movements, such as walking, running, opening a door or riding a bicycle. Imagine you are just in the process of doing it, or watch yourself doing it.

• Picture simple motion sequences involving the horse: you are leading the horse, you are tightening the girth, you are adjusting the stirrups and checking from the front that they are level, you are mounting.

• Then imagine (depending on your level of training): you are moving off, you are riding in walk and feeling your lower legs alternately coming against the horse and then being pushed off again slightly; you are doing rising trot, sitting, cantering on, and riding in canter.

Picture in your mind simple sequences of actions involving the horse, for example, leading, tacking up and mounting.

Imagine in detail that you are moving off and riding the horse in walk, then trot and canter.

• Here is an example visualisation exercise in which you 'see' and 'feel' a transition from trot to walk. Close your eyes (or leave them open if you find it easier), create the following image vividly and try to feel it intensely: you are riding in your usual school, with its markers, mirrors etc. Perhaps you can even smell a familiar smell (the horse's sweat, the material used for the riding surface), or maybe you can hear neighing or hoofbeats passing by.

You are riding on the left rein in working trot, feeling your horse pushing off energetically from behind, your lower legs gently moving in and out in time with the trot; the horse's back is swinging, and you can feel with your hands, on your ring-finger, a light, even, elastic contact with the horse's mouth.

Now your lower legs are pushing rather more actively towards your still, non-yielding hands, and at the same time your seat is being pushed elastically forward. Owing to the increased engagement of the hind legs, you can feel the horse carrying himself more, 'filling out' the area under your lower legs, his movement taking you

When recalling what you experienced during a transition, also create a concrete image of your usual riding arena.

Take advantage of every opportunity to visualise precise mental images of exercises.

with him. Next you make a soft transition into walk, and you are already thinking about the next phase, riding forwards in walk.

In practice, and particularly in test and competition situations, it is not possible to go all the way through the above, detailed, sequence.

Consequently, it is important to reduce it to a shortened formula which can be reiterated at any time, for example in this case: lower legs – hands – seat – lighter – walk.

• Gradually increase the length of the mental picture sequence until you can visualise a series of interconnected movements, such as sections of a dressage test, or a series of cross-country fences or show jumps. All the

Imagine you are making a soft transition into walk, and are already thinking about the next phase – riding forwards in the walk.

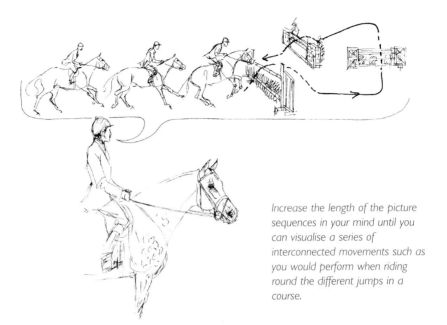

Increase the length of the picture sequences in your mind until you can visualise a series of interconnected movements such as you would perform when riding round the different jumps in a course.

time, talk yourself through your visualisation.

• Increase the demands of your mental exercises in accordance with your level of training, picturing different lessons, entire dressage tests, jumps, courses or rides.

Eventually you will be able to imagine a whole course of jumps.

REMIND YOURSELF I will always tell myself what I must do, and not what I must avoid.

4. Concentration

• Begin as described above, by imagining simple pictures and experiences. It is quite normal, when you first start to train your powers of concentration, to be repeatedly distracted by other thoughts, for example a recent argument, or a problem at work or at school.

• Do not try to suppress these disruptive thoughts altogether – they will simply recur more strongly. Instead, resolve to deal with them later. In your mind, write down the disturbing thoughts on a piece of paper and deposit the note in a 'problem box', promising to tackle the problems later. But do keep your promise, otherwise your subconscious mind will play tricks

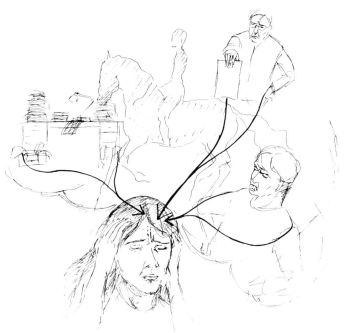

When trying to concentrate it can be difficult to shut out distracting thoughts.

on you at the next opportunity.

• Develop the film sequences in your mind into complex groups of movements such as dressage tests and courses of jumps. Practise running through these amid distractions: with music playing on the radio, with

headphones on, among other people who are talking or watching television in the same room, for example.

• Also visualise ridden exercises performed in adverse conditions, for example in bad weather, on poor going, in front of a critical audience, or

Mentally drop your disruptive thoughts into a 'problem box', with a promise to tackle them later.

With practice you can learn to run through your visualisation sequences amid distractions – with loud music on the radio, or with the TV turned up full blast.

Picture yourself riding in adverse conditions.

horse's reactions can lead you.

• If, when riding, you make a mistake, try to forget it straight away. Concentrate on the next exercise or the next jump. Make the best of it, even if it feels terrible! You should also avoid being distracted by thoughts of an exercise which comes later and with which you are having problems.

> **TIP** The most important exercise is always the one you are just about to do.

5. Positive attitude (self-confidence)

Are you the sort of person who is constantly grumbling at yourself, or who lives in a constant state of discord with yourself? If so, you should do everything possible to make peace with yourself and, basically, accept yourself. This does not mean, though,

surrounded by noise and flapping plastic flags. Imagine performing like this in a real competition, on which a lot depends. The greater your powers of concentration, the freer your mind and body will be to cope with unforeseen situations into which the

If you make a mistake, try to put it behind you straight away, and concentrate on the exercise ahead.

Say to yourself: "This is the right way," not "This is the wrong way."

that you should not want to be self-critical, nor to learn or improve.

• Consider the fact that there is no-one whose company you have to keep so constantly as your own. Perhaps through riding you will be able to make friends with yourself! Here are a few tips on how to go about it:

• Say, out loud if you are alone, "I did that well" if you have made a good job of something.

• Say aloud to yourself what your aim is, and that you are going to achieve it.

• Treat yourself fairly, and when you are judging an achievement, tell yourself what was good about it, and where you intend to make improvements: for example, "My horse stepped sideways slightly in the turn on the forehand. I must regulate more with the outside rein so that he steps more on the spot with his front feet."

• Tell yourself what was good and correct about an exercise, even one which went wrong.

• If, say, you have just ridden a dressage test and were not placed because you made some blunders, do not engage in a lengthy squabble with yourself because your horse broke into canter during the extended trot, or whatever. Instead tell yourself that next time you will get the horse straight in his body before the extension. Also tell yourself that in the rest of the trot he was consistently on the bit, and that the transitions were pretty good.

• Get used to expressing your aims positively, in terms of "I must" rather than "I must not". For example, in the leg-yield, do not think "I must not let my weight slide to the outside", but instead, "I must press my seat to the inside, with the movement".

TELL YOURSELF I will always express things positively: "This is the **right** way!"

• Start off in a positive frame of mind, so that you can analyse your faults profitably and with a clear head. Since you are no longer condemning everything outright, your mind is free to concentrate on the crucial details which will make for success in the future.

• Here's an example: for the last few months you have been getting on well with your horse, he has become

In training, you will sometimes have to contend with difficult working conditions.

calmer, and it takes twenty minutes of warming-up to get him to stretch forward and down onto the contact. He still needs to be more 'through', but you're getting there.

• Now consider this scenario: yesterday and the day before, you were really pleased with your horse and yourself. Today it's a disaster! What should you

When warming up, you must give yourself enough time, but not so much that you over-do it.

do? First, remember that the horse is a living creature, not a machine! Do not get upset; it is better to stop the session before any more damage is done and put the horse away. Everything will be all right in the morning!

• When things go wrong at a show, always ask yourself why. Was it due to external circumstances – were distractions by spectators, loud music or poor going to blame? You must decide, and try to incorporate similar circumstances into your training.

• Was it perhaps because you lacked concentration, or was your mental preparation unsatisfactory? You can work on this.

• Did the fault lie in the horse's preparation – maybe the exercises could be performed at home, in ideal conditions, but were not sufficiently 'established'? In this case, you need to work at improving and confirming them.

• Have you overdone your warm-up?

Recall the events and mood of a day when you were particularly successful.

Have you worked so hard that the horse has nothing left by the time you go into the arena? If so, you must think carefully about your warm-up technique and modify it.

• Recreate in your mind the events and atmosphere of a day when you were particularly successful. These will certainly contain important keys to your success.

• Find out what conditions are best for you at a competition, especially for the time when you are waiting to go into the arena. Is it noise or peace and quiet that you need? Some people prefer not to be spoken to, and spend the final minutes before the start completely cut off from the rest of the world, concentrating on what they have to do. Others find welcome distraction in talking to as many people as possible on every possible subject. One person will sit with headphones on, listening to music. Another will work himself up into an aggressive mood, because he needs to conjure up some 'fighting spirit' to get the best results.

• You must discover what conditions best suit you personally. You need self-confidence in order to be able to say to yourself: no matter what everyone else does or says, *this* is how it's best for me, and when all's said and done, only *I* can judge in what circumstances I can give my best performance.

> **TIP** Tell yourself: I will not let myself be put off or 'psyched out' by other people! It is for me and my instructor to judge what is good for me.

6. 'Self talk'

There are two areas which you can effectively influence through 'self talk', namely your emotional state ("I feel really good") and your behaviour (by telling yourself what you want or have to do).

*Practise self-discipline.
Say to yourself:
"That's it! Out!"*

a) Exercises for regulating the way you feel

• Begin with simple, everyday situations. For example, when you are having problems dragging yourself out of bed, say to yourself: "That's it! Out!" – practise overcoming your weaknesses!

• Or: sit in front of a blank sheet of paper in your typewriter, or a blank computer screen, and day-dream instead of working. Then tell yourself resolutely: "Now I am going to pull myself together and concentrate. When I have finished this task, I'll do

You can spur yourself on to greater effort by promising yourself a treat.

something nice, such as go to the cinema or out for a meal, or read my favourite novel." By promising yourself a treat, you will spur yourself on to greater efforts.

• At times when you hesitate or doubt yourself, remember what you have been trained to say to yourself: "Come on, you're good enough, you can do it!"

• Perhaps you have problems expressing yourself in words in front of other people. Tell yourself you can do it. Consider what you are trying to say, and put it into your own words.

Close your eyes briefly and say to yourself: "Breathe out steadily and fully – now I feel relaxed and ready for anything!"

• If you are trying to do everything possible to improve, and others are sapping your confidence, hold your head up high and say to yourself: "I am me. I am unique. No two people are the same. I know what I am going to do, and you can't put me off!"

• If before a competition you are nervous and 'up-tight', close your eyes briefly and say to yourself: "Now breathe out steadily, all the way – now I feel relaxed and ready for anything!"

Remember what you have been trained to tell yourself: "Come on, you're good enough. You can do it!"

• Or if you feel lacking in drive, dull and listless, you can goad yourself into action and incite yourself to peak performance by reminding yourself: "I'll show them! Today I will produce my best. I am in top form, and so is my horse!"

You can goad yourself into action and incite yourself to top performance by reminding yourself: "I'll show them. Today I'll produce my best. I am in top form, and so is my horse!"

KEY POINT   Tell yourself: before a competition, I can either goad myself into action or reduce my tension as required.

• If your confidence is at a low ebb and you are depressed because absolutely nothing has gone right today, force yourself to remember that yesterday or the day before, everything went much better. Say to yourself purposefully: "I can reproduce that performance any time. It was not simply a fluke; I can do it again equally well. Now I will remember exactly what it felt like and how I managed it."

• If your mind is elsewhere and you cannot concentrate because you have problems in your private life or at work. Shake them off! Say to yourself: "Just for this short time I won't think about them. Now I am going to ride, and nothing else. There is plenty of time afterwards. There is no point in

*Say to yourself:
"Now I am
going to ride
and I will forget
about
everything else
while I do so."*

trying to do everything at once. I'll shut myself right off from my anxieties. It *is* possible, damn it!"

b) Exercises for learning, reinforcing and improving skills

• For example, when moving off from halt, for as long as this is something new to you, say to yourself: "Press your lower legs against the horse, pushing yourself forward in the saddle, and at the same time yield with your hands." When you have learnt these aids and are using them correctly, you do not need to say or think anything further. You have made them automatic, and can 'retrieve' them whenever you need them.

• The format of your 'self talk' changes as the learning process progresses. The formulae become shorter and shorter, consisting more and more of key words, for example, "Pressure" (lower legs and seat), "lighter" (contact with the horse's mouth). This also results in your words being timed to fit your actions, because as you will notice, at

the beginning of the learning process, when you talk yourself through a movement in detail, it takes longer to say the words than to ride the movement.

• You also become more economical with words when dealing with any problems or faults which may have developed. For example, you have learned and are at home with the

If you have got into the habit of stiffening your left hand, eventually you will only need to say to yourself: "Left."

combination of aids for the transition from halt to walk (and also from walk to trot, and for lengthening the strides in trot). However, you have got into the habit of riding these transitions with your left hand fixed and stiff (there is always more of the bit showing on the left of the horse's mouth than the right). At first say to yourself, "Left hand lighter", but eventually shorten this simply to "left".

IMPORTANT Tell yourself: From time to time I will ask my instructor to help draw up 'personalised' abbreviated formulae for me to use for talking through the different exercises.

• Imagine that you are familiar with the aids for the turn on the forehand or

Your horse is falling onto the left shoulder and escaping sideways with too much bend in his neck. Your shortened formula for correcting this might be: 'Inside — outside.'

the leg-yield, but your horse keeps falling onto the outside shoulder, with too much bend in the head and neck, and running away sideways. You should be saying something like: "Inside leg – half-halt with your outside rein, by taking a slightly stronger contact and opening and closing your hand." Shortened form: "Inside leg – outside rein", and finally: "Inside – outside".

• In order to check your 'self talk', your instructor should ask you to speak out loud to start with, so that he can 'listen in'. Afterwards you will do the talking inside your head, where no-one else can hear it.

c) More exercises for learning and confirming riding skills
• **Half-halts:** Tell yourself in detail what you are trying to learn: "With my lower legs, and pushing my seat forward (as in upward transitions to walk and trot), I push the horse into still (non-yielding) hands for about one

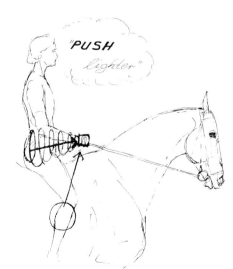

When riding half-halts and halts, eventually you will only need to say: "Push – lighter."

second (count: 'one, Mississippi'), then I lighten my hands and seat (i.e. stop pushing, sit passively)." Further half-halts are then performed as required. After practising this a few times while visualising the whole process in detail, shorten the formula to: "Forward into both hands – one, Mississippi – become lighter (hands and driving aids)". Finally: "Push – lighter".

• **Riding through corners:** First tell yourself in detail what you are trying to learn, and practise it in your mind as described previously. "Before the corner, flex the horse to the inside (how far before the corner depends on the horse). Then, with your inside leg against the horse, establish the bend. When the horse is exactly half way through the corner, lighten your inside hand, ride out of the corner, and straighten the horse." When you have practised this a few times and are familiar with it, the shortened form, "Flexion – bend – lighter (inside) – straight", is all you need.

Talking yourself through the light or half seat: "Legs (ankles and knees), upper body (shoulders forward slightly, seat just out of the saddle), hands (low)". Eventually, just: "Legs, upper body, hands".

• **The light or half seat** (for jumping or riding cross-country): Again, tell yourself what you are trying to do: "Take your weight on your stirrups and your knees. Bring your upper body forward slightly (the faster the pace, the further forward you bring your body), lift your seat just out of the saddle. Carry your hands low, possibly below the top of the horse's neck". Then move on to an abbreviated form: "Legs (ankles and knees), upper body (shoulders forward slightly, seat raised slightly), hands (low)". Finally, just: "Legs, upper body, hands".

• **Turning, when using the light or half seat:** To begin with, your 'self talk' runs as follows: "Put more weight onto your inside stirrup, and with your inside hand guide the horse in the

When riding through a corner: "Flexion – bend – lighter (inside) – straight".

Abbreviated formula for turns using the light or half seat: "Inside stirrup; inside rein asking, yielding; outside leg regulating."

direction of the turn and then yield; keep a contact on the outside rein, and use your outside leg to regulate or 'contain' the movement". For the final, abbreviated form: "Inside stirrup; inside rein asking, yielding; outside leg regulating".

KEY POINT 'Self talk' is an excellent medium for learning, for correcting faults, and for improving performance.

2

COPING WITH FEAR AND LEARNING HOW TO FALL

2.1 COPING WITH FEAR

Many people are afraid of horses and of riding – yet very few dare to admit it.

Fear has the natural positive function of self-protection and the preservation of life, so it is neither to be condemned nor laughed at. Fear warns us of danger; it is an alarm signal which we should take seriously.

Your horse provides a good illustration of how fear can save life and preserve the species. As a creature of flight he reacts to the alarm signal of fear by taking to his heels: he escapes by running away. Without this instinct of flight, the horse's chances of survival in the wild would be minimal, if not non-existent.

Our present-day domesticated riding horse also obeys this basic instinct. You can see this easily if you watch how this great big animal reacts to 'frightening' stimuli: he runs away – from clucking hens, plastic bags, fluttering leaves or an unfamiliar noise.

He tries to escape from anything unfamiliar – and which could be a danger – by fleeing. As a basic principle, this is very sensible. As a rider, you must understand and accept this, even if it is a nuisance or makes you angry, or if it leads you into unforeseen situations! The horse does not have the benefit of human reason, through which fear can be explained and usually overcome.

• As a human being, you can come to terms with your fear, by first of all facing up to it, then looking for the reasons behind it and trying to come to terms with it. It is possible that you will not overcome it completely, but you can learn to live with it. Above all, you can learn to distinguish between

TELL YOURSELF I realise that not only is my fear of genuine, non-imaginary dangers justifiable, but I should listen to what it is trying to tell me.

As a creature of flight, the horse reacts to 'frightening' stimuli by trying to run away from them.

serious negligence, and is taking a risk which he must avoid – yes, *must*, because he has the power to judge it as dangerous, and he possesses the faculty of reason and the capacity for self-appraisal.

• Never succumb to so-called 'dares', for example when someone tempts you to jump a certain fence, when just thinking about it makes your legs turn to jelly. The so-called 'courage' in this instance is nothing more than stupidity and mindless foolhardiness. It is more intelligent, and braver, to refuse. This also applies in the case where your instructor is inciting you to do something you are not confident about. You have a good reason not to comply, and should tell him. Maybe you or your horse are not yet ready, or you have not yet got your 'nerve' back after a fall, or you simply do not feel up to it that day. Moreover, if you demand things of your horse which are (as yet) beyond his capabilities, this could be construed as cruelty!

genuine, objectively perceived dangers, and imaginary ones, which you allow yourself to be 'talked into' through ignorance and lack of confidence.

• Real danger exists when you attempt to do something which you, or your horse, or both, are obviously not in a position to do. For example, a person who jumps a fence which is clearly beyond the capabilities of horse and rider, or of one of them, is guilty of

You can learn to distinguish between real and imaginary dangers.

• So never let yourself in for something (no-matter who asks you, or where!) which makes warning bells of fear ring inside you. There have been many accidents due, for example, to a rider allowing himself to be talked into going out for a ride or jumping a fence when he did not feel ready for it, and really did not *want* to do it on that occasion.

• The important thing is that you are honest with yourself about it. The next step is to be able to admit it out loud. You now know how to develop, through training, the necessary self-confidence!

AS A BASIC PRINCIPLE Tell yourself: I will only do what I really believe myself (and my horse) capable of. Anything else would be stupid and unsportsmanlike.

• The possible disastrous consequences of a student thinking he has to do as his instructor says and, for example, jump a fence in spite of his inner fear, have been demonstrated in practice by tragic incidents in which riders have been rewarded for their 'courage' by head injuries, broken legs, or even paralysis. So never let anyone persuade you that fear is nonsense. Take more notice of the inner warning signal than of all those convincing outside influences!

• For many young people, 'dares' hold an undisputed attraction. In such cases, the onus is on the instructor to decide what the student should be expected to do. He should take a firm stand against recklessness and overconfidence. He must make it abundantly clear to his students that 'dare devil' behaviour and 'showing off' can endanger them, their horses and other riders. Unsupervised jumping should be banned at all costs!

INSTRUCTOR'S TIP

Dares and dare-devil behaviour should be deterred from the outset.

• With adults, things are very different, especially if they have started riding relatively late in life. They often seem over-anxious, and should not be made to feel ashamed of it. They usually have good reasons for being reluctant to do something which they see as dangerous. They are more keenly aware of the risks, and often have a family and a job to consider; they simply cannot afford to have an accident.

Even if an instructor thinks that his student is well prepared for a new demand, he should never talk his pupil into doing something he (the rider) does not feel capable of. The very fact that his student is afraid is in itself a risk factor, and a potential recipe for disaster.

INSTRUCTOR'S TIP

Tell yourself: I will take seriously every sign of fear in my students. I will never talk them into anything they do not feel ready for, otherwise their worst fears are bound to be realised!

• It is perfectly understandable and natural that beginner-riders feel –

To beginners, a horse often seems enormous.

usually subconscious – fear or anxiety when faced with such a large and still very unfamiliar animal. This is particularly true in the case of city-dwellers, who, at best, have only ever been in contact with household pets.

• This fear is as normal as any fear of something strange or unfamiliar; it is simply the fear of the unknown. It can be overcome relatively easily through knowledge and experience.

• The beginner can master his fear through through intensive familiarisation with the horse, his nature and his behaviour; and even before starting riding lessons, through being 'around' horses, for example in the stable, grooming, leading, and getting as much contact with them as possible. Obviously this is only possible with quiet, reliable horses, which will inspire the necessary confidence. No self-respecting instructor should put a beginner on a nervous, jumpy or 'problem' horse!

• The instructor must also ensure that

the horse to be ridden is not too 'fresh'. Instead it should be lunged or ridden by an experienced rider beforehand.

• Obviously, the tack must also be suitable. The saddle and bridle must be in order, and fit perfectly. Risks, and so sources of fear, due to saddlery are unnecessary and avoidable.

• It goes without saying that a person starting riding lessons should wear an approved type of riding hat. A sturdy

An approved hat is a 'must' for learning to ride.

pair of riding boots (or at least boots which come above the ankle and have a heel) is also recommended for support.

• The instructor must also take care to introduce the student to the basics of horse management. It is better to do too much than too little in this respect.

INSTRUCTOR'S TIP

Tell yourself: I will do everything in my power to overcome or reduce fear. I will take care to avoid anything which could cause fear.

• However, as a student you can also do much to overcome your own fears. Before and after every movement and every action, picture in your mind exactly what you are trying to do, or what you have just done. This will enable you to train your 'feel'. You can practise running through these sequences in your mind wherever and as often as you like, without the need for a horse.

• By developing these skills, you will be laying the best possible foundations for putting them into practice in your riding.

• Also, carefully watch other people in their dealings with horses, and concentrate hard on imagining yourself in their place, as if it were you doing it.

• You may find some relaxation techniques useful (the 'shoulder-breathing' or facial exercises) before you make contact with the horse. Make sure you are concentrating really hard.

• Shut out everything else from your mind. Failure to concentrate can easily lead to carelessness and mistakes. Also bear in mind that nervous, fidgety behaviour can be dangerous in that it can unsettle the horse and frighten him.

• Perhaps you simply need to bolster your confidence by telling yourself: "I have learned such and such and done it a few times, so now I know how to do it!" or "I don't care if other people are standing there smirking, I'll manage."

• It may be that your fear is based on bad experiences in the past. Perhaps when you were a child you were bitten or kicked by a horse, or you are still haunted by a fall you had years ago.

• You need to analyse these fears, discover the cause, and try to gradually overcome them with the above-mentioned exercises and the professional help of a good instructor. It is important that you do not simply talk yourself out of your fear, or allow yourself to be talked out of it ("Come on now, don't be such a coward!" or "You wimp, there's nothing to it!"). Only after you have accepted your fear and the causes for it, and taken steps to combat it meaningfully and systematically, will you finally be convinced – not bullied into thinking – that there is no longer any reason for it.

• Have the courage to admit your fear to yourself and to others and to refuse flatly to do what you are afraid of.

REMEMBER Fear is a risk factor, which unsettles not only the rider, but the horse as well, with danger as a direct consequence.

• Since fear is communicated to your partner, the horse, who is a living creature, it is even more dangerous than in other sports.

• Also, impress upon your mind that courage is not to be confused with foolhardiness, or mindless dare-devil behaviour, which may be synonymous with sheer stupidity! When you have managed to allay your fears by training your mental skills, and assessing your abilities realistically, you will be the best judge of what you are, and are not, capable of. You will also be sufficiently self-assured not to have to prove anything to yourself or anyone else by responding to (reckless) 'dares'! However, fear is not only a risk factor in itself. It can also 'paralyse' you and persistently block the learning processes, because it monopolises your concentration and energy.

• It may be that you are by nature a rather nervous person, who does not have much confidence in yourself. By doing mental exercises (e.g. relaxation, concentration, building self-confidence), you will put yourself in a position to counteract this. You should also avail yourself of the mány benefits of 'self talk', as discussed earlier.

• You may simply be afraid of making a fool of yourself in front of others, and feel the need to have your skills acknowledged by them. You may be worried because your friends and colleagues are present, along with some of your critics, and you are keen to impress them.

• Maybe you have discovered that it is your self-confidence in particular which needs to be boosted – in which case you

Mental exercises can help you to overcome your nerves in the presence of spectators.

Tell yourself: "I can put into practice what I have learned so far."

49

know from your training how to tackle this problem.

• Often, it is not really too difficult to say to yourself: "I can put into practice what I have learned so far. I'm actually pretty good." It may help to adopt a defiant attitude: for example, mentally give the victory sign or raise a clenched fist.

TIP FOR COMBATING FEAR

Tell yourself: I will confess to my fear, discover the causes, and combat it by using the mental skills which I now have at my disposal. I now know enough about what I am doing to be able to have some confidence in myself! I will not let myself be talked into things which go against my inner convictions.

• If you are the sort of person who tends to lack self-confidence about most things, not just sport-related ones, then you must work at viewing yourself positively overall. You may not be one hundred percent successful! However, you can learn to look upon individual achievements positively, and make yourself conscious of the fact that you have achieved something. It would be nice if small successes in riding helped you in other areas too!

• However, do not confuse fear with 'stage-fright', the normal excitement before a ride or a competition. Stage-fright can be a very useful stimulus to action, and usually evaporates when you have been in the arena for a few seconds. After all, if you have practised the mental skills in Chapter 1 you know you can regulate this excitement,

either by curbing it or giving it full rein. You will have learned to control yourself and your reactions. And you know that without that inner 'buzz', top performance is not possible.

TELL YOURSELF   I know that excitement can be positive if I have it under control. Moreover, it is indispensable on occasions when a special effort is required.

• Perhaps you are simply over-anxious. You meet all the criteria: preparation and equipment are as good as they can be (the latter includes a hard hat!); you are not overestimating your own ability, nor that of your horse; you are riding under the professional supervision of your instructor. In short, there is no logical, realistic reason why you should be afraid.

• Nevertheless, you are still frightened! What you must do is bolster your self-confidence, get yourself into a positive frame of mind. Say to yourself emphatically: "I can do it. There is no danger." Also say to yourself: "My horse can feel my fear, and that is in itself potentially dangerous. I shall ride as if I were not frightened." Visualise the whole thing (the jump or whatever) in as concrete a form as possible in your mind (but without making it look bigger than it is!). You may be allowing yourself to believe in dangers which are simply not there! Pull yourself together: force yourself to discard all feelings of fear and self-doubt – and just ride. The exercises in relaxation and concentration will help you here. Get yourself into a confident mood,

If you meet all the criteria, there is no realistic, logical reason to be afraid.

and overcome your fears through activity.

AS A BASIC PRINCIPLE Tell yourself: I'll find the courage, because I am ready to do it! I am good enough. I have practised and learned how to prepare myself mentally. I can visualise the situation clearly and realistically in my mind, as often as I want. It's ridiculous to think that I can't do it!

2.2 LEARNING HOW TO FALL

by sports trainer Klaus Chmiel

You have just been learning how to handle fear, and how to decide whether to listen to it or to conquer it.

Fear of falling off the horse is perfectly natural. You and your instructor can do much to avoid falls, and also to minimise the dangers if you do fall off. The most important

requirements are set out below:

• Adoption of the protective measures required by the official competition rules for your sport (e.g. wear a suitable hard hat).

• A well-trained horse with a suitable temperament.

• General familiarity with horses, and some basic 'horse sense'.

• Self-discipline and caution in all dealings with horses; avoidance of recklessness and overconfidence.

• Physical fitness (as for any other sport).

• Concentration on the task in hand.

The two types of exercise which are the subject of this section have until now, unfortunately, not had sufficient attention paid to them. They are:

a) Warming up the muscles before you get on the horse – a preparatory measure which is taken for granted in other sports.

b) Exercises for learning how to fall, which enable you to separate yourself promptly from the horse, and then to roll away.

Don't be fooled: in spite of all the safety measures, no-one is completely immune from falling off an animal which, as a creature of flight, is easily startled and prone to react unpredictably at times. It doesn't only happen to beginners, but to experienced riders as well! Through adequate preparation, though, you can considerably lessen the risks involved. You should, therefore, become thoroughly proficient in the exercises described below. They enable you to fall correctly, and therefore safely. The rider who has this ability to react correctly is less afraid of falling, and the confidence which this gives him is often enough in itself to make him fall better and more safely.

INSTRUCTOR'S TIP

Enlist a qualified sports trainer to introduce students to these most important exercises correctly. They will consider it worth the money when they see how sensible and useful they are.

Warm-up exercises just before getting on the horse

• If possible cycle or walk to the stables (put your riding boots on just before mounting!).

• Jog for five minutes before riding.

• Get the horse ready, groom him, saddle him, leave him standing tied up, and do some stretching exercises.

Sequence of exercises to prepare muscles, tendons and ligaments

*Hold onto something, bend your knees fully with your heels on the ground. **Effect:** Stretches the muscles of the legs and seat.*

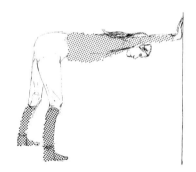

*With your legs wide apart, bend from the hips with your hands against the wall. Push your upper body down, with arms outstretched. **Effect:** Stretches the legs and shoulders, and also the chest muscles.*

*In a walking position with the forward leg against the wall, bend your upper body over your forward leg. **Effect:** Stretches the legs and the trunk.*

'Lunge' position: left then right leg stretched back with the upper body upright. **Effect:** Stretches the legs and the hip extensor muscles.

Lean against the wall, stretch one leg out behind you, and bring your hips forward. **Effect:** Stretches the calf muscles and the hip extensor muscles.

Lean backwards against the wall, and with both hands pull one leg up against your body. **Effect:** Stretches the muscles at the back of the leg and seat.

Facing the wall, raise one arm to shoulder-height and place against the wall. Turn your head and outer shoulder away from the wall. **Effect:** Stretches the chest muscles.

Stand with your back against the wall and stretch your arms upwards. **Effect:** Stretches the back and shoulders.

Sitting on a chair, bend your upper body forward with your legs the width of the chair apart. **Effect:** Stretches the muscles down the back of the body.

Sit straight on the chair and stretch your arms upwards. **Effect:** Stretches the muscles of the back and shoulders.

Exercises in falling

Exercises in falling should be preceded by a careful warm-up programme and performed on a suitable floor surface. Do not try these exercises without a knowledgeable helper, and preferably under the supervision of a qualified sports trainer, perhaps from a local gym or fitness centre.

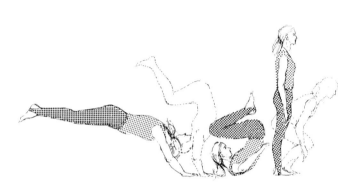

Forward roll – *from the squat into the squat.* **Note:** *With your hands parallel and shoulder-width apart, and fingers pointing forwards, place your weight evenly on both hands. Put the back of the neck and the shoulders onto the ground, pulling the head right in against the chest. Follow this with a forward roll from walking, and later a forward roll from running.*

Flying roll – *Work up from the squat to attempting a flying roll from standing position, then from walk, and finally from running.* **Note:** *A powerful spring into the roll is necessary – place the hands (parallel) on the floor only after the feet have left the ground. To start with, never practise without a helper, who should kneel on the floor and support the back of your neck.*

Forward roll from a standing position, *onto the right and left side. In this exercise, owing to the sideways element, the body contacts the floor diagonally.*

Take a step forward with the left leg.

Incline the upper body forwards and downwards, support the right hand on the floor (the hand should be level with the forward leg), so that the feet and the hand on the floor form a right-angled triangle.

Let the left arm hang down vertically under the centre of gravity of the body, with the eyes looking towards the right upper arm.

The roll is begun by pushing off lightly with both feet. You roll over the hand, the upper arm, forearm and shoulders, diagonally over the back towards the seat.

Finally you roll onto the right side of the body, and cushion the impact (the procedure is reversed when you start with the right foot forward). An even better way to disperse the energy is simply to continue the roll back into the standing position.

This may all sound really difficult when you read it. In practice, and with expert instruction, all will become clear. The important thing is that you know how to fall in the best way possible from the horse when the need arises, and to get clear straight away. It is better that you master one type of roll than none at all.

FALL TECHNIQUE When it happens for **real,** remember the following: quickly get your feet out of the stirrups, allow yourself to fall free, rounding your back as you do so (chin on your chest), then roll away.

3

BEGINNINGS

3.1 CHOOSING A RIDING SCHOOL

You have decided to learn to ride, something you have perhaps dreamed of doing for years.

• Your first consideration is to find a suitable riding establishment. Do not spare yourself time or trouble when making your choice. Your decision will determine whether your expectations will be fulfilled, or perhaps surpassed, or whether you will end up annoyed and disappointed.

• Since you are just starting to ride, buying a horse of your own is not yet an issue (not until you have about 100 hours in the saddle behind you should you start thinking about this). So your choice is limited from the outset to establishments which have school horses or horses they hire out, and which offer riding instruction for beginners.

• Before deciding, look carefully at as

many riding schools as possible, obtain written information, and ask staff and riders about all the things which are of special interest to you. Collect material for comparison, and leave as little as possible to chance.

• Naturally, **cost** cannot be ignored: how much do private and group lessons cost?

• Also of relevance is the **distance** from your home or place of work to the riding school. The time taken and the costs involved also need to be included in your considerations. However, it may be worth travelling further to a riding centre that you like than to opt for one which is 'on your doorstep' but which is less attractive.

> **POINT TO CONSIDER** Is it worth travelling the extra distance to go to a riding school which you prefer?

• Take a careful look at the **facilities.** Are the indoor school and outdoor arena well maintained? If your ultimate dream is to be able to go for pleasant rides in the countryside, do not forget to ask about the availability of hacking.

• Also take a look round the **stables.** But do not simply go poking around as if you owned the place – ask for permission first! Things to look out for are whether the horses look well fed and well cared for, whether they have contact with each other and with the outside world, whether they are in loose-boxes (as opposed to tied up in standing stalls), and whether the stables are well ventilated, light, dry, and provided with fresh, clean bedding.

• Also enquire about the **staff.** Is there an instructor with a suitable, nationally recognised qualification (in Britain these are issued by the British Horse

Society or Association of British Riding Schools; in the United States many instructors are registered with the American Riding Instructors Certification Programme), and does he or she give instruction to beginners – or is this left to trainees, working pupils or other 'experienced' riders?

Ask to be shown around the stables and look to see if the horses appear well fed and cared for.

• Ask if you can watch some of the lessons, in order to judge the **instruction.** Leaf through this book: you will find clues as to what good, effective instruction should consist of.

• Ask whether, and to what extent, **theoretical instruction** is provided.

• Ask yourself if the 'tone' of the place appeals to you, both in and outside the school.

• The **ages** of the riders might also play a role in your decision. Not all adult riders are happy to be in a group

Look carefully at the facilities and watch some of the lessons.

In a well-run yard, the horses will look happy and interested.

consisting mainly of children and young people. Nor do most young people relish the thought of being permanently in the company of members of the older generation!

• Are you interested in **organised events** such as social outings on horseback, hunting, taking tests, in-house competitions, visits to big equestrian events, riding-club dances and other social functions? Make enquiries about these.

• Above all else, be honest with yourself about your **individual needs.** There is nothing to be ashamed of if these are not exclusively sport- or performance-based. It is quite acceptable for you to want to make contact with other horsy people, whose company you can enjoy.

• Have the courage to find things out, by talking as much as possible to the instructor, the other staff, and the riders.

IMPORTANT Glean as much information as possible! This will shield you against disappointment and wasting your money.

3.2 FIRST CONTACT WITH THE HORSE

• You have found your riding school and booked the first lesson. You can use the time in between to gain some general experience of horses. This applies especially if you are a city dweller and have not grown up in the country, so you have never before had any contact with horses.

• Maybe such great big animals inspire you with all too much respect, and you are basically afraid of them. Or maybe, on the other hand, you have no reservations, and intend to step boldly and fearlessly into the fray.

• Both attitudes, nervous and

If you dream of going out for rides in the countryside, ask if the riding school caters for this.

excessively bold, are based on lack of knowledge, and are incorrect and actually dangerous.

• The horse is not a piece of sports equipment like skis or a tennis racket. It is a living creature with its innate behaviour patterns, its needs, and the reactions proper to a creature of its kind. You need to get to know and understand all these things in order to be able to 'tailor' your own reactions to them.

• Of course, you can get hold of good books about the horse's nature and about dealing with horses generally, and you will do this if your interest and anticipation are great enough.

• However, it is important that you put into practice and consolidate the theoretical knowledge you have gleaned.

• Take advantage of opportunities to handle and be around horses in the stable and elsewhere. However, this does not mean that you should get in the way of the stable staff when they are working, or that you should pester people with questions when they have their hands full doing something else!

• What you can do is watch carefully. And no-one will mind if, choosing the right moment, you ask politely to be shown how to groom. Any true horseman must be able to groom and look after his horse. It also provides you with an opportunity to get to know your 'sports partner' in depth, and handle him correctly.

• You may also be allowed to help with mucking out and feeding, or someone

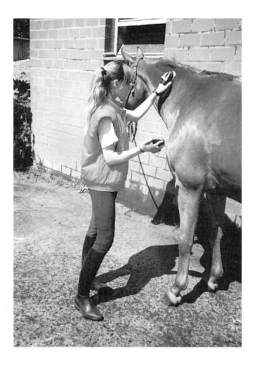

You may be allowed to groom your horse before you ride him.

bridled. This is a service to the customer which busy people are glad of. If you are a beginner, ask to be shown at some point how to put on the saddle and bridle correctly, and how they should fit. You will certainly be able to use these skills at some later date. Moreover, you will definitely enjoy it, and it is another opportunity for you to gain important hands-on experience.

• All this may sound very time-consuming, but it does not need to be. We are talking about approximately an extra 20 minutes, or perhaps half an hour, dedicated to handling the horse, on top of the time you spend riding. You can touch your horse, observe him, talk to him, do a few jobs – in short, get to know him.

• You will soon realise how important this contact is for you, and will notice how, as your confidence grows, inhibitions and uncertainty are gradually overcome, and you become more 'natural' and self-assured in your dealings with the horse.

may let you take out their (quiet!) horse to graze, or to lead around the yard to dry it off. All these activities help to get you used to handling horses and teach you to understand them better.

• In some riding schools, the student finds his horse ready saddled and

You may also be allowed to help with mucking out and feeding.

Take every opportunity to handle horses and get to know them.

• There are numerous, graded tests for riders to work for at different levels of competence, such as, in Britain, the Pony Club and Riding Club tests, or in the United States there is also the Pony Club and the National 4-H Council tests, which are not primarily orientated towards professional riding careers, and in which great emphasis is laid on 'horse sense' and general horse knowledge'. You might one day like to take these tests, which serve as a tangible measure of your progress. Even more important, the more confident you feel in your dealings with horses, the more you will enjoy your sport.

AS A BASIC PRINCIPLE It is a requirement of your sport that you are completely 'at home' with horses and in a horsy environment.

Every contact with the horse fosters understanding, trust and confidence.

3.3 LEADING

Leading the horse is one of the basic handling skills. Normally you will be taught it before your first lesson by your instructor or another, experienced, rider. However, you can help yourself by finding out the details beforehand, and making yourself familiar with what is involved, so that you do not feel out of your depth when you first try it.

• Your horse is already saddled and bridled. Stand on the left ('near') side of the horse, take the reins over the horse's head, hold them with your right hand just behind the bit rings, and hold the end of the reins in your left hand. Position yourself just behind the horse's eye.

• Stirrups must be run up the leathers (i.e. not hanging loose), and if side-reins are fitted, they must be unclipped from the bit rings and fastened up out of the way.

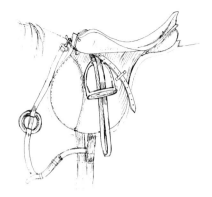

For leading, the stirrups must be run up the leathers, and it is essential that side-reins, if fitted, are fastened up out of the way.

• As you move off, remain in the same position relative to the horse. Do not pull the horse along behind you! Encourage him to walk on by talking to him or clicking your tongue gently. But do not look him in the eyes. Most horses stop immediately if you make eye contact. Also, it is better if you keep looking straight ahead when negotiating small obstacles and when

If someone else is leading a horse in front of you, ensure that there is a safe distance (about one horse's length) between you.

DISTANCE!

problems arise. If the horse rushes forward, calm him with your voice and steady him with short pulls on the reins followed immediately each time by a loose rein. If someone else is leading a horse in front of you, a 'safe distance' (about one horse's length) between you must be strictly observed. Neither you nor your horse must be in range of the hind feet of the horse in front.

• You must also be aware that excitable horses should not be handled by beginners! If you do not feel in control, you should not feel ashamed to ask your instructor or an experienced rider for help.

• Take every opportunity to see how other riders lead their horses. Go over and over the process in detail in your mind (you can also do this at home, on your bicycle or on the bus).

• Keep asking other riders to let you lead their horses. If you ask them nicely, they will be only too pleased to let you.

> **TIP** Tell yourself: I can make all early handling and skills easier for myself by practising them beforehand (and afterwards) in my mind. In this way I will gain confidence, be able to avoid faults, and be able to concentrate all my energies on the actual lesson.

3.4 MOUNTING AND DISMOUNTING

Here again, picturing and practising the process exactly and in every detail in your mind will enable you to perform it more quickly and correctly

If there is a wooden horse available, you can practise mounting and dismounting as often as you like.

in practice. When you come to do the actual lesson, you will be less hesitant, and your mind will be free to deal with it.

• Watch other riders mounting and dismounting, and picture yourself in their place.

• If there is a wooden horse available, you can also use this to run through both exercises in practice, as often as you want, and at the same time you will be sparing the real horse!

• Before **mounting** (which, like leading, is done from the left), check that the girth is tight. Otherwise you and the saddle together could slide under the horse's belly! When tightening the girth, clamp the left rein in your left elbow so that the horse cannot get away.

• Then take both reins in your left hand. They should be fairly taut, so that you have a contact with the horse's mouth.

• While you are doing this, and throughout the exercise, the horse must stand absolutely still. If at any point he

Before mounting, take both reins in the left hand, keeping a contact with the horse's mouth.

becomes restless, break off the exercise, make the horse stand again, and go back to the beginning. Be strict on this point, since it is unnecessary and discouraging for your first attempt at getting on a horse to end in you being deposited unceremoniously on the ground because your horse has suddenly departed! Do not keep on trying for too long. If there is not already a helper in attendance, ask politely for someone to hold your horse while you get on.

• Stand with your back to the horse's head, put your left foot in the stirrup, and take care that your toe does not dig into the horse's belly or side!

• Place your left hand, with the reins in it, on the front ('pommel') of the saddle or on the horse's withers, and hold the back of the saddle ('cantle') with your right hand. Push off strongly with your right leg, and swing it over the croup (without touching the latter), and sink softly into the saddle – this is important, since if you crash down onto his back, the horse may take fright and bolt.

• Put your right foot into the right ('offside') stirrup. To start with, you can look at what you are doing, and use your hand to guide the stirrup. Later you will be able to do it 'blind' and without thinking. This is simply a matter of practice.

• Once you are on, sit upright in the saddle in the normal position (see later). If you have already learned on the lunge how to hold the reins, take up

Push off strongly with your right leg and swing it over the croup.

If you have been taught how to hold the reins, take them up now in the riding position.

your reins as if to ride forward.

• To begin with, all this may sound really complicated. However, you will soon find that, in practice, you quickly get used to doing it, and it finally becomes almost automatic. Mental training can make the learning process easier and quicker.

• Especially in the beginning, it is helpful if you can commit the main points to memory: keep a contact with the reins – the horse must stand still – sink softly into the saddle – immediately put the right foot into the stirrup.

• Before **dismounting** at the end of the lesson, first take both feet out of the stirrups. This is very important, since otherwise you could be dragged with your left foot in the stirrup if the horse takes fright, runs away, or jumps sideways. This could lead to a serious accident.

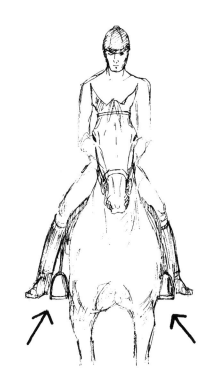

Before dismounting, it is very important to take both feet out of the stirrups.

To dismount, rest your hands on the pommel and swing your right foot cleanly over the croup.

• Rest your hands on the pommel, swing your right leg over the croup, without touching the croup with it, and slide down on the left side, landing softly with your knees bent – softly, because you can really hurt yourself by landing hard.

• Lastly, unclip the side-reins, if fitted, and fasten them up out of the way, run the stirrups up the leathers, loosen the girth, and stand next to the horse ready to lead him.

• Here again, pick out the main points: both feet out of the stirrups – land softly – run up the stirrups and loosen the girth.

At the end of the lesson run the stirrups up the leathers, loosen the girth, ready to lead the horse away.

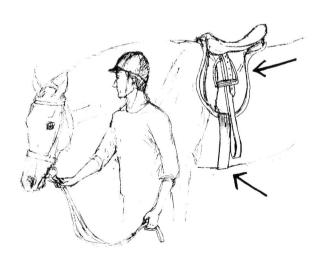

CHAPTER

4

THE FUNDAMENTALS OF RIDING

4.1 METHODS OF TEACHING AND LEARNING

This chapter revolves around the following issues: the aim of the learning, the method of learning, any problems which may arise, suggestions for instructors, lessons learned from past experience, and examples of our way of doing things.

1. Aim

We show you with words and pictures **what** you can learn, e.g. what the turn on the forehand looks like, and what you must do in order to be able to ride it; or what aids you should use, for example, to move off from the halt, or to ride a transition from walk to trot. This subject matter, i.e. 'what' you learn, is in accordance with the principles of classical horsemanship.

2. Method of learning

Then you see **how** this learning can be facilitated by mental skills: by training your 'feel', by picturing the exercise in your mind, and by talking it through with yourself. This method is more effective than previous methods.

Relaxation, concentration and a positive attitude are necessary for learning each movement. If you encounter problems, you can do the appropriate exercises to resolve them (see earlier). These skills are applied in the same way to all the exercises, and in the following pages are only discussed in detail in special cases.

You must see something in order to be able to learn it: this maxim applies to all riding skills. You must watch good examples of the movements – in the school, on TV or on video – and do so often enough to be able to visualise exactly what you want to learn.

IMPORTANT Tell yourself: I will visualise myself riding the movement I have been watching; I will imagine it exactly.

Special tips for easier learning

We also tell you things which will make it easier for you to learn each exercise correctly, for example, the best way to learn how to strike off into canter is to practise sitting into and 'feeling' the canter strides. Another example of a special tip is, during a private lesson, to ask your instructor to ride through the new exercise for you on 'your' horse, and to 'tune' it to the correct aids.

3. Problems which may arise

Here you learn what you can do if things do not work out even though you have done everything as we have suggested.

Basic questions to ask if things do not work out

Ask yourself if all the preconditions have been met:

- Have you reached the necessary level of training to be able to ride, under professional instruction, the movement in question? (You need to ask your instructor this.)

- Does your horse meet the requirements, or is he easily distracted, for example by outside influences?

- Does your horse feel 'normal' – normal for him, that is (temperament taken into account)? Or, for example, is he more high spirited than usual because he has just had a day off?

- Are you in a fit state to learn – or, for example, has your learning capability been impaired, perhaps by psychological strain or nervous exhaustion?

- Are you physically fit, that is, not sick or run down?

- Is your instructor a reasonable person, or is he an objectionable type who indulges in shouting and personal insults? In the latter case, you should consider replacing him forthwith!

- Are the weather conditions normal, or is it, for example, very hot or very cold?

- Are you comfortable or, for example, are your breeches tight across the knee?

If there are no problems in these areas, you should question and perhaps improve your **mental skills.** Ask yourself:

- Am I tense or anxious? – If so, go back to the relaxation exercises you have learned.

- Have I developed the necessary 'body awareness'? – Run through the exercises again (you do not need a horse!).

- Is the motion sequence I have formed in my mind of this exercise accurate and retrievable? – Ask your instructor to go through it with you.

- Is lack of concentration the problem? – You can practise and improve this at any time.

- Do you lack confidence in your ability to do the exercise; do you say to yourself: "I can't do it"? Or do you allow yourself to be 'psyched out' by other people, who always know better or even laugh at your attempts? – Remember that you have practised **thinking positively** and bolstering your self-confidence. Repeat the mental exercises.

■Have you tried every way you know of talking yourself through it? – Try everything again.

Of course, the fault may lie with the horse. Perhaps he has 'switched off', or is simply not finely enough tuned. In this case you should ask your instructor to ride him, and then afterwards let you experience what it is supposed to feel like.

Often, if you work through all the other possibilities, you will not need to resort to this measure. You will be surprised to find how infrequently the problems are due to the horse, and how much more effectively you can solve them by yourself.

4. Suggestions for the instructor

Finally, some suggestions for the instructor. For your benefit we have gone into somewhat greater detail, because we feel you should be given the opportunity to learn and use this method, which will bring enormous benefits to both you and your students. The beginner-rider in particular needs the knowledgeable support of a good instructor in order to practise and use mental training.

If you are open-minded and receptive, you will find in this book numerous suggestions which will make the lessons more interesting and rewarding not only for your students, but for you too. You will find that your new approach brings your clients greater satisfaction and enjoyment.

A few basic tips and lessons learned from experience

• Keep a check, when you are giving

practical instruction, on how much talking you do and what you say (usually we talk far too much!). Try to say only things that will do some good. Do not tell the student things he already knows. Not only is this superfluous, but it prevents him concentrating on himself and the horse.

• It is also unnecessary and irritating to shout or speak too loudly. Speak just loudly enough to be heard by the person you are addressing.

• For discussions and longer explanations, call the student (or students) to you, and ask him to halt. It is simply asking too much of most people to ride and listen to long explanations at the same time. In so doing you are completely wasting your energy.

• Refer back to and follow up every correction you have made. Tell the

The instructor should make a real effort only to say things which will be productive.

For longer explanations, the instructor should call the rider to him and talk while he is halted.

The best way for the instructor to address a group of riders is to line them up in front of him in a semi-circle.

Always try to finish on a good note. The instructor should repeat the exercise until the rider achieves at least some small measure of success.

student whether he is now doing it (the movement or exercise) better or correctly. Get him to repeat the exercise until he achieves at least some small measure of success. Always try to finish on a good note ("That was better that time").

• Tell the rider what he should do, and not what he must not do. Avoid negative instructions such as "Don't draw your heel up", or "Don't hang your head", etc. Stand him next to you and simply ask: "Can you feel your ankle/your head position"? "Don't tense up" is completely meaningless, and will cause the rider to tense up even more!

• Try to work less with corrections and judgements. Get the rider to experience what it **should** feel like (see below). In this way you will avoid the inhibiting influences of negative self-criticism ("I've done it wrong again! I'm stupid, I'll never learn it"). This

simply leads to loss of confidence and lack of self-esteem, without which nothing can be learned or achieved.

• You must be able to communicate to the rider what things should feel like.

• Get the student to express in words what he is experiencing. Only if he does this can you check to what extent he

*When instructing, tell the rider what he **should** do, and avoid negative instructions.*

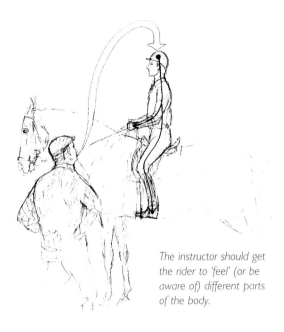

The instructor should get the rider to 'feel' (or be aware of) different parts of the body.

has digested what has been learned, and how secure he is in this knowledge.

• Instead of making superfluous corrections, ask the rider to 'feel' the parts of the body in question.

• In order to be able to do so, he must learn to experience things consciously, to commit what he experiences to memory, and to reproduce it.

• Impart these skills to him through the correct, methodically carried out procedures, and the acknowledgement of positive results (with praise!) – tell him immediately if his seat or aids, or the horse's paces and position, or his jumping, were good.

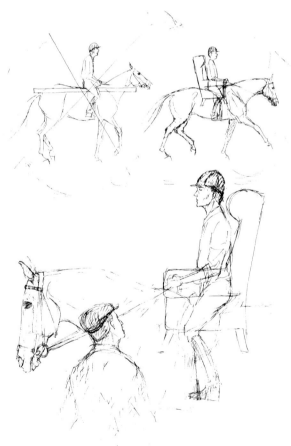

Through mental rehearsal the feelings experienced become blueprints, which can be recalled over and over again.

• Get the student to commit to memory the feeling he experienced when, for example, his horse was uniformly bent throughout its length, or was loose, or on the bit.

• Through mental repetition, these experiences will become blueprints, permanent models which can be recalled over and over again. Reinforce them by saying to the student: "Imagine exactly the feeling you just had, as if you were actually experiencing it again." If you think it will help, get the student to do this at the halt with his eyes closed.

• When he repeats the exercise in practice, he should experience again the feeling he has pictured in his mind. Ask him if this is the case, and compare what he says with what actually happened. If the feeling was not right,

go through the whole process again in a shortened form.

• Once the feel of what has been experienced has become established in his mind, get the student to practise in different conditions, and then finally in more difficult ones.

• Let the student get on with riding new or imperfect exercises without you criticising them. Instead, ask him what he felt.

• With badly performed movements which have become automatic and ingrained, do not start by trying to correct them. Build up new, correct movements in their place, and do nothing to bring the old ones to mind.

Instructor-student relationship
• In the very first lesson, the student

The instructor should try to build the student's confidence – "You can do it at home, so you can do it in any other arena in the world".

must promise you that he will tell you immediately if he does not understand something exactly.

• Adopt the use of some key words, which only the two of you need be able to understand, e.g. instead of the description of a halt, use "push" (meaning ride forward into still, non-yielding hands), and "lighter" (meaning lighten/ease your hands and your driving aids).

• Try to adopt and instil into your student a positive attitude, and be encouraging. If he says to you, for example: "In competitions I just can't ride a serpentine", you reply "You can ride it at home, so you can ride it anywhere – in any arena in the world!"

• It is often necessary to ride a student's horse in order to fine tune it to the aids again. Try to be honest, however: it is good for the instructor to try to help the student, but not so good if he simply wants to show off!

• Consider your relationship with the student. You should not simply be

The student should be encouraged to be an active partner in the lesson and not just passively take orders.

'spoon-feeding' him. He should take an active part in the proceedings, and should become progressively more responsible for monitoring his own actions. Your instruction will be better and more effective if you make your student a partner in the discussion, a partner who is enthusiastic and eager to learn.

• However, do not throw out the baby with the bath water! Do not try to change radically everything you have been used to doing: not everything about it is wrong! The new method will simply help you to achieve your aim more easily. You can gradually try more and more things out, and go on to do more when you feel you are having some success.

• If you have to do six to eight hours' instructing per day, it will be quite impossible at first for you to use the new method throughout. Everyone who has been in this situation knows that there are times when you have to go into 'automatic' mode, otherwise you would not be able to cope. However, you can adopt this training system progressively, intermingling it with your existing teaching method. You will soon notice that you achieve more with your students, that they are getting greater satisfaction, and moreover, that your work is more interesting and can even be fun!

4.2   THE BASIC SEAT

I. Aim
Position: The foundations of the seat are the two seat bones and the crotch.

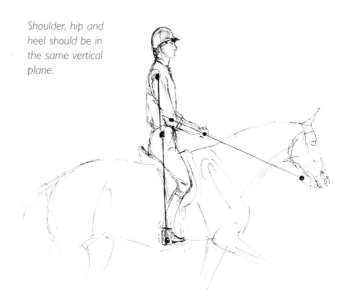

Shoulder, hip and heel should be in the same vertical plane.

These should be deep in the saddle, and pulled as far forward as possible. When riding straight ahead, the weight should be distributed equally on these three points. The shoulder blades should be drawn back slightly, and the upper body should be upright. The head should be carried erect, with the eyes looking straight ahead. The upper arms should hang down vertically and without tension, with the elbows next to the hips and free from stiffness. The line through the forearm, the back of the hand and the rein, to the horse's mouth, should be approximately straight. The hands should be closed with the knuckles lined up straight in a vertical position, and the thumbs on top 'like a roof'.

The thighs should be well 'let down', and lie flat against the saddle, with the knee as low as possible, and the lower legs far enough back for the shoulder, hip and heel to form a straight line (when carried normally). The lowest point is the heel; the toes point only slightly outwards.

The seat described in the text is the ideal, from which there may be slight variations.

THE RIDER'S SEAT

The seat described here is the **ideal.** Slight deviations from this may be necessary to accommodate 'conformational' peculiarities of horse and rider.

Suppleness: What is important is that the correct external characteristics

You absorb the movement with your pelvis and thighs.

of the position are not achieved at the expense of looseness. You should commit to memory that the following six joints must be free from stiffness and tension: shoulders, elbows, wrists, hips, knees and ankles.

> **REMEMBER** Suppleness takes precedence over correct outward form!

In the horse, the centre of movement is the back; in the rider, the combination of the pelvis and thighs plays this role: they swing forward with the movement of the horse's back, allowing the seat to maintain a supple contact with the saddle. It is wrong for the oscillations of the movement to continue visibly all the way up the spine, and then stop abruptly at the base of the neck. This results in an unsteady upper body and a bent, nodding head.

You should absorb the movement in your pelvis and thighs, while your upper body remains straight and free from stiffness. Not until you can sit quietly and softly in this way are you in a position to give the aids correctly – and only through this latter skill will you one day experience that special satisfaction and enjoyment which only this partnership between Man and horse can give.

2. Method of learning

The following can be practised even before your first lunge lesson:

• **Mental skills:** You can practise all the mental skills discussed earlier, so extensively on the ground that it will

Impress on your memory pictures of riders sitting correctly. (Dr Reiner Klimke.)

be relatively easy for you to use them when you are on the horse. Place special emphasis on relaxation exercises and exercises aimed at developing body awareness and mental imaging skills.

• **Visualising a correct, supple basic seat:** As with everything which you set out to learn, it is important that you can form in your mind beforehand a clear picture of exactly what you are trying to achieve. Impress on your memory pictures and/or photographs of riders who are sitting correctly. Before you do so, ask an experienced rider, or better still your future instructor, whether the picture you are thinking of using is really a good example. Imagine that you are this rider, with every part of your body in the same position and

carried in the same way. Try to emulate all the details. Hang the picture of your role model on the wall, in a position where you will notice it.

• Watch films and videos featuring good riders. Try to 'ride with them', and train your ability to recall the movements in your mind. Take special notice of the pelvis and upper legs (is the rider sitting softly and supply?), the hands (is there a soft, elastic contact with the horse's mouth?) and the lower legs (are they lying quietly and supply against the horse's body?). Ask advanced riders to point out the essentials to you.

• Watch as many riding lessons as possible. Notice what corrections the instructor makes. Imprint on your mind the things he praises, and try to reconstruct in your mind what you have seen.

• If your future instructor has time, ask him for explanations, and answers to your questions.

• Also ask him if any theoretical instruction is planned, or could be arranged, prior to the first ride.

• Watch novice riders receiving instruction on the lunge. Listen to what the rider is told to do, and try to go over it afterwards in your mind.

• Read through the following section on training the seat on the lunge, so that you can see what good instruction on the lunge should be like.

• When you are being lunged, talk to your instructor about trying out the above suggestions. Do not be afraid to ask! Put into words what you are feeling, and what you have experienced, and ask if it is correct. Ask him during the walk or halt intervals to listen to what you have to say, and to check the picture of the exercise which you have in your mind. Also, if you are afraid, have the courage to admit it – there is nothing to be ashamed of!

• It is important that you do all the above at an early stage, before a small unnoticed fault develops into a habit. React to the first signs of a problem – it makes it much easier to deal with.

SPEAK UP   Speak out and say what you need, ask any questions and express any fears.

3. Suggestions to the instructor for position training on the lunge

• Before the first lunge lesson, offer the student some **theoretical instruction:** you can use pictures, films and videos to demonstrate the basic seat and to draw attention to the main points. Get the student to form an image in his mind of what he has seen, and to ask questions if there is anything he is unclear about.

• It is a good idea to start off by practising mounting, dismounting and the correct seat on a **wooden horse**.

• Give the student the opportunity to watch a lesson, and encourage him to ask questions.

• We are assuming that at least the first five lessons will be on the lunge. Obvious requirements are a suitable, quiet horse which is not too 'fresh', suitable equipment, and a saddle with the lowest point of the seat in the centre. Using a vaulting roller for beginners, instead of a saddle, also gives good results.

• Instruction on the lunge begins with **exercises at the halt.** The student now has the opportunity to practise, consolidate and refine on the horse's back the mental skills he has developed beforehand. By contracting and relaxing the various muscles, he tunes in to the main muscle groups as he has learned to do, and also experiences for the first time the contact with the horse's body. At the slightest sign of nervousness or uneasiness, incorporate some relaxation exercises.

• The actual lunge work begins in

walk, without the student holding the reins. He may or may not hold on to the saddle, depending on what is required, and on his aptitude. Here again, if he tenses up or shows signs of anxiety, relaxation exercises are helpful.

• Take plenty of time over **training the seat and position in walk.** With adults in particular, long, intensive training in walk is recommended. This should last until the student has lost all traces of fear, and is able to sit softly into the movement and balance himself. Here, the same principle applies as to the early training of horses: time spent at the beginning is an investment, which will be repaid with interest later!

• Another advantage of the mental training method is that extensive training in walk does not become monotonous either for the instructor or for the student. There are plenty of opportunities to make the rider 'conscious' of his body, and to reinforce and monitor this awareness or 'feel' through mental rehearsal. Through this 'feel', the student experiences the horse's movement. He feels, for example, how his pelvis and thighs accompany the movement of the horse's back, and how his legs are alternately drawn to and pushed away from the horse's body.

• The instructor should then ask the student to describe what he can feel when his legs are resting against the horse without tension. He then gets him to do, as a back-up, an action replay in his mind of what he felt. This will also provide the foundations for riding the horse forward in walk correctly and in time with the strides, a

skill which often causes problems even for experienced riders!

• **Training the seat in trot** should be done just as carefully, and should be interrupted by frequent periods of walk, to give the rider the chance to do relaxation and other mental exercises. Lungeing in trot is also done initially without the reins, and with the rider either holding on or not – the main thing is that he feels happy and remains free from stiffness. First he learns rising trot, then he experiences what it feels like to sit softly in sitting trot, though the latter for only short periods at a time to start with: never continue so long that the rider becomes visibly distressed, tense – or simply in need of a rest! Frequently changing between rising and sitting trot helps develop looseness (which also makes for a secure seat), and trains the feel for the movement.

• In **canter** too, suppleness and freedom from anxiety are the main considerations – whether or not the

Lungeing in trot should be interrupted by frequent periods of walk to give the rider a chance to do relaxation and other mental exercises.

rider is holding on. Never continue the canter for too long, and in no circumstances go on for longer than the rider wants to or can cope with!

IMPORTANT Look out for the slightest sign of anxiety or uneasiness. Reduce your demands for the moment. Try not to force things.

• **Holding the reins** on the lunge is the next step, and there is only any point in the rider doing so if he is sufficiently confirmed in his seat to be able to concentrate on his hands. The hands should be reasonably independent.

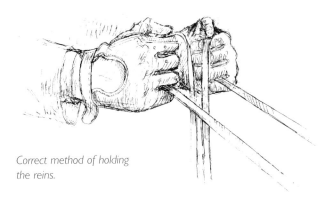

Correct method of holding the reins.

• The **contact with the horse's mouth** is practised again at the halt. Allow the student to feel the horse's mouth at the halt, and reinforce this by holding the bit rings in order to make the contact easier for him to feel.

• Training the rider's contact with the horse's mouth in walk serves a very important function. The rider should be made to practise this intensively and really take it in. Your part in helping him might go something like

this: "Can you feel the movement of the horse's neck? Allow it, go with it. Yes, like that! Halt and recall the feeling that you had. Can you feel it? Now ride the walk again exactly like last time." Through this process you will succeed in teaching him a valuable skill. The problems of many experienced riders are due to the fact that they failed to learn from the outset how to go with the movements of the horse's neck. The consequence is a restricting hand, i.e. a hand which 'blocks' the movement, and which can cause the walk to degenerate into a pace-like gait (i.e. to tend towards a lateral two-time gait).

• In all the basic gaits, lay special emphasis on the rider 'feeling' the movement, expressing what he feels in words, and having a supple seat, one that is free from stiffness, and comfortable. This will provide him with the foundations for the correct application of the aids without it being necessary to tackle this as a separate issue.

REMEMBER Only if something can be expressed in words can it be altered, and so improved.

• **Dismounted mental preparation and review** are indispensable. 'Homework' reinforces and gives greater depth to what has been learned, and to the student's ability to monitor it. Relaxation exercises are also useful, particularly when problems arise.

• When the student has developed the mental skills, and has received

The instructor should allow the student to feel the contact with the horse's mouth at the halt, and if necessary, facilitate this by holding the bit rings. This applies to all levels of training, and not just to beginners.

The correct leg position is also best taught by helping the student to 'feel' it.

thorough, correct training on the lunge, riding off the lead behind another, steady, horse will not present anything new, and is a logical, harmonious progression.

• The examples which follow, and which we use in our day-to-day instruction, are intended to give riders and instructors the confidence to explore new possibilities.

The 'feel' for the correct foot position is taught by getting the rider to feel the difference: **Top:** *Heel too high;* **Centre:** *Heel too low;* **Bottom:** *Correct.*

4. Experiences and examples of trying correct faults

Every instructor and every student knows how ineffectual corrections can be, even if repeated! With mental training, more is achieved with less effort than with the conventional methods.

Both instructor and student are probably familiar with the following frustrating, depressing situation:

Here is Mrs So-and-so on her horse again: she's been riding with her toes down for three years now... nothing's changed! Not that she does it intentionally; she tries so hard to get everything right, it's just too bad she can't do it!

Her instructor, Mr Bloggs, has made up his mind, after his outburst during the last private lesson, to be patient this time. "Heels down!" Mrs So-and-so pushes her heels down. "Yes, that's right!" Mr Bloggs stares spellbound at Mrs So-and-so's heels. How long will it last? A quarter, or even half way round the arena before they go up again!

This is just one example: there are endless similar cases which could be quoted. How can it be that the earnest efforts of two, intelligent adults can meet with so little success?

There are two main reasons why instructor and student are driven to despair.

One is that the student is, so to speak, 'pre-programmed' in the belief that failure is inevitable, and is tensing up in anticipation of this.

The other reason is that, because she

has not been trained in body awareness, she cannot tell whether her heels are up or down; she only becomes aware that they have risen up when she is next corrected.

In a very similar case, the use of the new method with one of my students resulted in an outstanding success. Firstly I asked: "Can you feel your ankles?" After a while, and after moving her ankles, she replied: "I can now, but only the right one." A little while afterwards, she added: "Now I can feel the left one too." By drawing the student's attention to her 'feel', and so enabling her to check the position of her heels for herself, I had solved the problem. In a very short time, all I had to say to her was "Can you feel your heels?", and her foot position was correct.

This does not mean that success is always guaranteed in this way. I often find that it is better not to keep referring to the part in question. The question "Can you feel your ankle?" soon becomes reminiscent of the old command "Heels down!" and so loses its value and becomes negative in its effect. In these cases you will achieve much better results if you get the student to describe before or afterwards the feel, for example, of his lower leg against the horse's body.

The following tips may assist you in trying out different ways:

• Ask the student to practise feeling the difference (on or off the horse), for example, between opening and closing the hands, hanging the head and then holding it normally, leaning the upper body forward (jumping seat) and then sitting in the normal upright position,

The instructor should encourage the student to become aware of the position of the pelvis.
Top: *Hip joint locked (pelvis to rear).*
Bottom: *Hip joint more mobile (seat forward).*

stretching the arms forward and then holding the elbows against the body (or against the sweater, T-shirt etc.), sitting with the hip joints locked (pelvis to the rear) and then with the hip joints mobile (seat forward), opening and closing the knees, riding with the heels up and then down.

• Combine your seat and position training with your training of body awareness or 'feel'. Make fewer criticisms and corrections, and instead get the student to describe what he can feel: "What do your head, shoulders, elbows, fingers, hands, hip joint, upper leg, knee, lower leg, ankle feel like?"

• Make less use of long, logical explanations (reasoning). Instead, rely on looking and feeling. The advantage of this is that complex sequences of movements are first experienced as a whole, instead of being dissected in the mind and then finally, laboriously, being put back together again. Thus you are focussing the rider's attention from the outset on the most important

means at his disposal, his 'feel'. Long explanations only serve to prevent him experiencing this.

• Remember how many different explanations you need to make in order to describe, for example, the aids for strike-off into canter (you may also have found this when you yourself were under instruction, or when you were reading up on the subject afterwards). "The inside leg sends the horse forward, the outside leg (a hand's breadth further back) controls the quarters, the inside seatbone is pushed forward slightly, the inside hand, by yielding, allows the first canter stride to come through," etc. In order to create the right effect, you must do all these things not only within the space of one short moment, but also in the right measure and harmoniously!

• It is hardly surprising if this method of portraying the process makes it harder, rather than easier to learn. You will make it so much simpler for the student if you focus on his 'feel': "Picture quite clearly in your mind what you feel during each canter stride, and how your body responds to the movement. Simply sit in the same way, and do the same as you do in every canter stride: this is the best aid for striking off into canter."

• Make up your mind to avoid direct corrections and comments as far as possible. These are external interventions which serve to inhibit 'feel' rather than help to develop it.

• This does not mean that you should change your style of instructing abruptly and completely. This is unrealistic, especially if you put in a lot

The instructor can teach the student to practise the aids for the strike-off into canter by concentrating on 'feeling' each canter stride.

of hours instructing. However, what you can do, and what is recommended, is that you experiment with the new method by carefully trying it out bit by bit in conjunction with your normal teaching methods. In this way you can gradually convince yourself of its effectiveness, and soon you will not want to be without it.

4.3 THE AIDS AND THEIR EFFECTS

I. Aim

What are the aids? Aids are physical signals through which we communicate with the horse: you tell your horse, by means of your legs, weight and hands, what you want him to do.

As an **auxiliary aid,** the **voice** can also be used, for appropriate purposes and in moderation (for commands on the lunge, or on occasions in ridden work, for calming or encouraging the horse). Other auxiliary aids are the whip and spurs, which are used to back up the driving aids.

Aids are an international 'language'. Through them, you can communicate with horses throughout the world, provided they have been 'schooled', i.e. received some dressage-type riding horse training.

Make it your aim to progressively refine your aids until they are hardly visible – or, ideally, not visible at all – and using them requires a minimum of physical effort. Ultimately, your success depends on the finely tuned, smooth coordination of your aids. First, however, you must be familiar with the individual aids and their function.

What is traditionally described as a **leg aid** is, more exactly, the elastic pressure of the **calf** or **lower leg** against the horse's body. Make sure that your legs, when driving the horse forward, push in time with the movement (i.e. in a walk-, trot- or canter rhythm): they must not remain clamped against the horse!

There are three kinds of leg aid: forward-driving aids, sideways-pushing aids and regulating aids. For

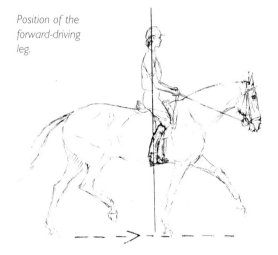

Position of the forward-driving leg.

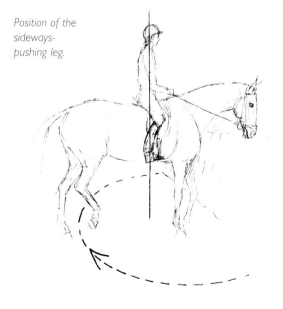

Position of the sideways-pushing leg.

Leg position for regulating the quarters.

the forward-driving aids, in walk and trot, both legs are in the normal position (shoulder, hip and heel form a perpendicular line). In canter, only the inside leg is in this position. The sideways-pushing leg (for example in the turn on the forehand or leg-yield) is in the same position as the forward driving leg. The 'regulating' leg (for example in the turn on the forehand, leg-yield or canter) is positioned about a hand's breadth further back than the sideways-pushing leg.

Weight aids consist of the action of your weight on the horse's back. There are three different kinds of weight aid. The first consists of putting the weight equally on both seat bones in conjunction with pushing the seat forwards slightly in the saddle, for example in upward transitions to walk or trot.

The second consists of putting the weight on one seat bone, for example when turning, or striking off into canter.

The third involves easing the weight off the seat bones, thereby making yourself lighter and so easing the

weight off the horse's back. In doing this you transfer your weight more onto your upper legs and position your body slightly in front of the vertical. You do this when riding in the light or half seat (for jumping and cross-country riding), when riding young horses or horses which have a sensitive back, or in the rein-back.

The **rein aids** enable you to act on the horse's mouth with your hands via the reins and bit. They can be roughly broken down into 'regulating' (limiting, containing or 'guarding'), 'non-yielding', 'asking' and 'yielding'. An 'asking' or a 'non-yielding' rein aid must always be followed by a 'yielding' rein. The 'asking' aid includes a wide range of variations, from the almost imperceptible opening and closing of the hand (comparable to squeezing out a sponge), or the turning of the hand from the wrist, to taking the arm back from the elbow (when there should still be a straight line from the elbow, through the hand, to the bit).

KEEP TELLING YOURSELF Use non-yielding or asking rein aids only in association with driving aids, and remember to yield frequently.

Preconditions

For the rider: Before you start to use the aids on the horse, you must have learned on the lunge to keep your balance and to sit independently of the reins.

For the horse: He must be sufficiently established in his basic schooling to respond well enough to the aids so that the rider can learn how to gauge the aids correctly.

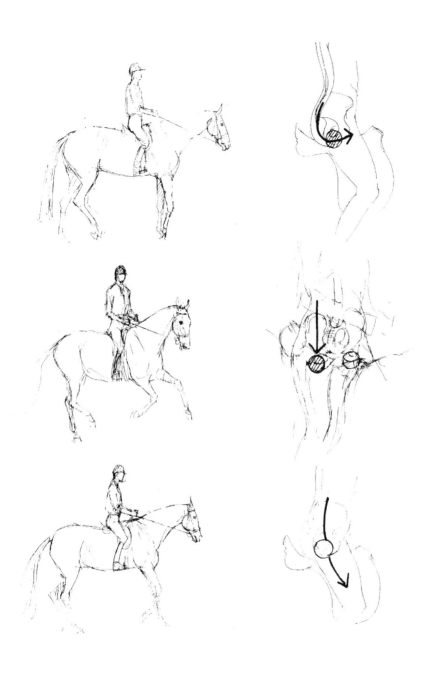

Putting the weight on both seat bones.

Putting the weight on one seat bone.

Easing the weight off the seat bones.

2. Method of learning

• Have enough lunge lessons for you to feel confident and secure in the three basic gaits.

• Ask your instructor to position your legs correctly against the horse at the halt, and imprint on your mind what it feels like.

• Keep training your body awareness so that you can feel exactly where your lower legs are, and what they are doing.

• Ask your instructor to hold the reins behind the bit rings in order to convey to you the feel of a sensitive, even contact with the horse's mouth, and of a slow taking and giving action (in that order, with an 'asking' rein aid followed by yielding rein aid).

• Putting the weight equally on both seat bones (at the same time pushing the seat forward in the saddle) is practised in conjunction with the driving (leg-) aids. Feel how your pelvis comes forward. On no account must you hollow your back, which would serve to lock the hip joint and so prevent its movement.

• Practise all the aids in their basic form, and the interplay of leg and rein aids: practise them in different intensities, and practise all the different variations and combinations. In conjunction with the forward-driving aids, practise using a yielding, a non-yielding and an 'asking' rein. As you do so, push your seat elastically forward in the saddle.

• This will enable you to experience the basic reaction: when you push and yield, you send the horse forwards; when you push and hold, you check the horse.

• Discuss with your instructor a formula to help you to do this, for example this could be: "Push (drive with legs and seat), lighter (hands)".

• Practise in your head, including without the horse, the many possible combinations of aids, and their synchronisation.

• Practise refining your driving aids by frequently pausing between them. Your aim should be for the horse, in an active (medium) walk, working trot and working canter, to maintain the pace solely in response to the natural in-and-out movement ('breathing') of your legs accompanying the strides. Driving the horse continually only serves to make him go 'dead' to the aids, and puts unnecessary strain on the rider!

REMEMBER Only push as much as necessary - aim to get an immediate response.

3. Problem-solving – a few examples

PROBLEM

Your horse is not going forwards; he is not responding sufficiently to your driving aids.

TIPS

Check if your legs are elastically accompanying the horse's movements, or if they are rigid and 'clamped' against him.

• Sharpen your horse's responses by using the whip at the same time as your legs (or, at a later stage of training, the spurs), and then repeating the aid without the whip or spur.

• Ask your instructor to get on the horse and 'retune' him to the aids.

• Check your seat. Maybe do some training on the lunge. You can remind yourself of what it feels like to sit supply, without the added complication of having to apply aids.

• Do some relaxation exercises.

• Ask your instructor if you can ride another horse who is more responsive to the aids.

PROBLEM

In the leg-yield or on a circle, your horse falls onto the outside shoulder and escapes sideways.

TIPS

• Check that your outside rein and outside leg are performing their regulating or 'guarding' function.

• Check that your inside hand is yielding sufficiently. This fault can be recognised by the fact that more of the bit is showing on the inside than the outside!

• Ask your instructor to demonstrate again how much contact you should have with the horse's mouth.

PROBLEM

You have problems with the canter strike-off (depart): your horse comes above the bit or 'explodes'.

TIPS

• Check your weight aids: they may be too strong or abrupt. Transfer more of your weight onto your upper leg during the strike-off (depart).

• Rehearse the aids for the canter

After a poor strike-off, come back to trot, get your horse on the bit, and only then try the strike-off again.

strike-off (depart) by practising sitting into and 'feeling' the canter strides, perhaps on the lunge.

• Do not simply keep going after a bad strike-off (depart). First get your horse on the bit again in trot, and then, using finely tuned aids, try the strike-off (depart) again.

• Ask your instructor to monitor what you are doing.

> **IMPORTANT** Tell yourself: Having the right feel for applying the aids effectively is fundamental to everything I shall learn in the future. I must be strict with myself from the beginning, because once faults become established, they are difficult to eradicate!

4. Suggestions for the instructor

• Retuning the horse to respond to correct, sensitively applied aids (either you or another, good, rider can do this) is the best and most direct way to get the rider to experience the correct 'feel'.

• During the lessons which follow ask the student if he can remember exactly what it feels like, for example, to yield with his hands (but without letting the reins hang in loops) from a light, sensitive contact. Or ask him to recall how it feels to halt by pushing the horse into a still, non-yielding hand.

• Check that the rider's 'feel' is correct by asking him to tell you when he experiences it again. Give the student a 'refresher' if the memory has faded.

• Try different ways of doing things before you begin to doubt yourself or your student (or both!).

5. Example of how to try to eradicate an ingrained fault

Using this system, the student makes a greater verbal contribution than he would under conventional teaching methods, and this enables the instructor to see things through the student's eyes, and so to find and remove the causes of the faults more easily.

A peculiarity of learning a movement is that, in comparison with learning something rationally, it is extremely demanding in terms of time, energy and instruction. However, once the movement in question has been learned and has become automatic, it becomes a part of us, as it were. For example, once you have learned to swim or ride a bicycle, you never forget how to do it. Likewise, in riding, you do not 'un-learn' anything you have learned, even if you go for years without doing it. This is, of course, a great advantage; but the disadvantage is that wrongly learned movements are equally difficult to 'un-learn'!

Instructors and students are equally aware of how difficult it is and how long it takes to correct ingrained faults in the rider's position and in the application of the aids. Even when you think you have cured it, it tends to reappear the next time the rider is in a test or competition situation.

For example, through working with

jumping horses I had got into the habit of performing flying changes using the light or half-seat, with my weight off the horse's back. Later, when I became more involved with dressage horses, this habit of standing up slightly in the stirrups caused me serious problems, especially in tempi changes. It took a long time to eliminate the fault completely, and I would definitely have found the process easier if I had read the book *The Inner Game* by tennis trainer, Timothy Gallwey. This author describes how much more difficult it is to correct wrong movements than it is to teach new ones. As a result I now appreciate the importance of not referring to what the rider is doing wrong when he gives the aids, but, instead, of describing the new, correct way of doing it.

By applying this knowledge, I have achieved amazingly rapid results with some of my students. For example, I would notice that in the flying changes they were making the same mistake as me, or they were putting their weight too far back. If at this point I had said: "Sit down," or "Don't stand up", I would have reminded the student of his bad habit, and so caused it to reappear. Instead, I said: "While you're in right canter, just do another strike-off, into left canter" (or vice versa). To my astonishment, the seat, the aids and the change were flawless. I had managed to avoid the fault by not referring to it; instead I had conveyed to the rider how to apply the aids correctly. Furthermore, I was also reminding him of a straightforward strike-off into canter, an exercise he was familiar with, and which was automatic to him.

4.4 HALF-HALTS

I. Aim

What are half-halts?
Pushing the horse forward with the legs and weight into anything other than a yielding hand (i.e. into a regulating, non-yielding or 'asking' hand) is called a half-halt. A downward transition from one gait to another, or to a halt, is obtained by a series of small half-halts in succession.

A half-halt is used in conjunction with all the other aids, and can vary greatly in its exact form and its intensity, depending on the level of training, and the obedience and sensitivity of the horse. For example with young horses, or horses which are sensitive in their backs, there is no active use of the rider's weight, or else a mere 'suggestion' of a weight aid is given by pushing the upper leg forward. As a rule, the half-halt lasts from one to two seconds, and ends when all the aids become lighter or passive.

In the authors' opinion, it is the synchronisation of all the aids during half-halts which is the key to good riding. How, and how well, they are performed are essential criteria for gauging a rider's ability. You cannot learn to do good half-halts straight away, or at the first attempt. The important thing is that you understand the correct technique as soon as possible. You will spend a long time improving and refining it!

What are half-halts for?
You perform half-halts for the

following purposes:

• to obtain downward transitions from one gait to another or to halt;
• to decrease the strides, e.g. to change from medium to working trot;
• to improve or maintain the halt;
• to flex the horse laterally, or change the flexion;
• to improve the horse's ability to 'let the aids through';
• to make the horse more attentive, e.g. prior to a new exercise or a transition;
• to improve or maintain the collection.

One or both hands may be active, depending on the effect you are trying to achieve. For example, if both hindlegs are required to engage, as for a transition or a halt, then both hands are active. If you want to act on one side only, for example to obtain lateral flexion, or to prevent the horse falling onto the outside shoulder, then you perform the half-halt on one rein – the appropriate inside or outside rein.

2. Method of learning

• Have one or two private lessons in order to master the basic technique.

• Constantly train your 'body feel', so that you can feel exactly where your lower legs are, and what they are doing in relation to your hands.

• Practise all the aids in their basic form, and the coordination of leg and rein aids in their different combinations and intensities: practise sending the horse forward alternately into a yielding and a non-yielding hand, while at the same time pushing your seat elastically forward in the saddle.

• In this way you will feel the basic response: pushing and yielding serves to send the horse forward; pushing while the hands stay put serves to slow the pace.

• Recite out loud to your instructor what your inner voice is saying in your mind. For example this could be: "Forwards (push with legs and seat), one Mississippi (approximately one second), lighter (hands and driving aids)".

• Try making your aids for the half-halts barely perceptible so that your

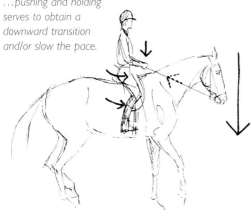

Pushing and yielding serves to send the horse forward…

…pushing and holding serves to obtain a downward transition and/or slow the pace.

horse can just understand you, and practise variations and different intensities. Take care not to use these combined aids too strongly – especially the weight aids.

• Practise these small half-halts to obtain a downward transition or halt, but also within a gait to maintain or improve the horse's attention, 'throughness', bend or collection. (Ask your instructor to explain about these qualities if you are not sure about the terms.)

TIPS Tell yourself: It is better to do several small half-halts than one big one which the horse resists.
Also, my horse must remain 'round' and on the bit.

3. Tips for solving half-halt problems

PROBLEM

The horse resists the half-halt, for example by hollowing his back and raising his head.

TIPS

• Use more discreet aids, and preferably give several small half-halts.

• Use your body awareness to gauge how actively you are using your weight. Try to transfer some of your weight onto your thighs.

• Check the duration of your half-halts – they should not last much more than a second.

PROBLEM

Your horse is going against the contact (coming against the hand) in the half-halts.

TIPS

• Feel what you are doing with your hands. Perhaps you are bringing them back too far, too hard, or for too long. Remember to lighten the hands quickly enough.

• Try to feel if you have the same pressure in both hands, or if you are using one hand more strongly than the other.

4. Suggestions for the instructor

• The best way to communicate to the rider the feel of a sensitive, even contact with the horse's mouth, of the non-yielding rein aid, and of the asking and yielding movement, is for you (the instructor) to take hold of the reins behind the bit rings and demonstrate this.

• It is a good idea to impress upon the student from the start the rhythm and sequence of the half-halts: "Forwards (push towards your hands, approximately one second), lighter (hands and driving aids passive)". Repeat this a few times and get the student to say it back to you. In the lessons which follow monitor the rider's progress by asking him to repeat his formula in the shortened form while you watch him perform the half-halt.

• Even afterwards, when the student has learned the correct feel, he should continue to comment on each half-halt.

• You will obtain good results if you keep suggesting to the student that he gives small half-halts and, if necessary (depending on the horse's reaction), that he should use his weight aids more carefully.

Tell yourself: When training and monitoring half-halts I will not spare any effort. I will impress upon the student that several small half-halts are better and more effective than one big one. I can demonstrate this to him, in particular in the transition from trot to halt.

5. Experiences and examples of trying to correct faults

While monitoring and correcting the application of the rein aids, I have found here again that it is far more effective to create new 'feels' and movements than to refer back to old faults.

The widespread practice of 'sawing' on the reins, which consists of pulling the bit, gently or not so gently, from side to side through the horse's mouth, is on the whole to be condemned. When I have encountered this, many students, when asked to keep their hands still, did so only briefly. Others simply carried on undeterred. When I asked them if they were now using the reins correctly, they answered with an unqualified "Yes"! I got my message across only by taking hold of the reins by the bit rings and getting them to feel a steady, even contact with the horse's mouth, and then asking them to go over this in their mind and concentrate on what they felt, as if they were still actually experiencing it.

The following experience shows how disastrous it can be to refer to old faults, even if this is done in a positive sense, in the form of a compliment. At our riding school, I had been aware for some time of one student who had a habit of pulling on the inside rein and not using the outside one. The first time she came to me for instruction, I asked if she had any particular problems. She promptly admitted: "I know my outside hand is really bad. Lots of instructors have already told me."

I said nothing, and instead took hold of the reins behind the bit rings and got her to feel the correct way to flex the horse laterally, via a calm, soft, asking and yielding on the inside rein accompanied by an elastic contact on the outside rein. She then went over and practised this in her mind, and afterwards I was amazed to see that the fault had disappeared completely. Furthermore, the result was a lasting one. Because I was so impressed, I said to her one day: "Your outside hand is really good now." I could not believe my eyes: the old fault immediately reappeared. To get rid of it, I had to repeat the process of making her experience the right feeling and practise it in her mind.

So it is definitely more effective to ask: "What can you feel in your hands/legs/ankles [or whatever]?" than to make any kind of reference to a fault, and so remind the student of it. Reminders seem inevitably to make old habits reappear. When I ask students what they can feel, I also find out important details, such as what sort of contact the lower leg has with the horse, or if the pressure on the fingers is not equal. I can then communicate to the rider and impress on his mind what it **should** feel like, without mentioning the old faults at all.

It can happen, however, that old faults reappear in difficult situations or when unforeseen problems arise. Typically, as one student commented: "It feels like when you were holding the reins, but only when my horse is going well." This shows that she was only 'programmed' for an ideal situation. So it is important to include problem situations in the mental training: even in problem situations, the student must be in a position to picture the movement as vividly as if he were actually doing it.

INSTRUCTOR'S TIP

Tell yourself: I can communicate to the rider via his 'body feel' what the movement should feel like if done correctly, and if possible I will not mention faults directly.

CHAPTER

5

INDIVIDUAL EXERCISES

5.1 TRANSITIONS

I. Aim

In this section you will learn how to ride transitions from one gait to another, and within a gait (increasing and decreasing the strides).

Downward transitions, halting, and decreasing the strides

If you want to change down from one gait to another (e.g. from canter to trot, or from trot to walk) or do a transition to halt, you use the half-halts described in the previous chapter. The same applies if you want to decrease the strides, for example from lengthened strides in trot to working trot, and later, from medium trot to collected trot.

In the early stages, the aids for changing down, halting and decreasing the strides consist simply of checking the horse with both hands. The voice can also be used to help steady the horse as required. You should use this soft asking and yielding action – at first without the driving aids – in the

following cases:

a) if you have not yet mastered the art of riding half-halts;

b) if your horse is not yet on the bit, and so is not yet supple enough in his back to let the half-halts through.

Upward transitions into walk and trot

The aids for upward transitions into walk and into trot are the same: you push with both legs simultaneously, pressing the thickest part of the calf briefly against the horse's body, and at the same time you yield with both hands and push yourself elastically forward in the saddle.

To prepare for the **transition into canter**, flex your horse to the inside, perform a half-halt with your outside hand, and place your outside leg a hand's width further back. For the actual strike-off, the aids are as follows: the inside leg drives the horse forward, the outside leg is held in what we call a 'regulating' position, and the inside hand yields to allow the inside hindleg to spring forward.

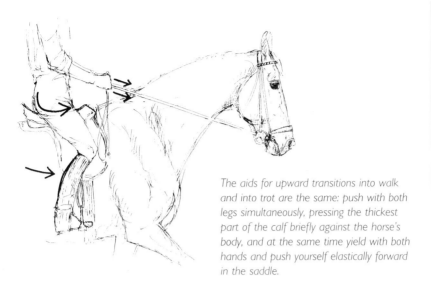

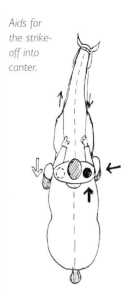

Aids for the strike-off into canter.

The aids for upward transitions into walk and into trot are the same: push with both legs simultaneously, pressing the thickest part of the calf briefly against the horse's body, and at the same time yield with both hands and push yourself elastically forward in the saddle.

Maintaining and increasing the strides

In order to keep the horse going in the basic form of the gait, or to increase the strides, you must know the correct driving aids, which are different for each gait, and are always accompanied by yielding the hands. The intensity of the aids depends on the horse's keenness and sensitivity.

In **walk** your legs push alternately, and act on the hind foot which is being picked up.

In **trot** you push with both legs simultaneously, always at the point when a hind foot is leaving the ground. In rising trot, you push at the point when you sit down in the saddle.

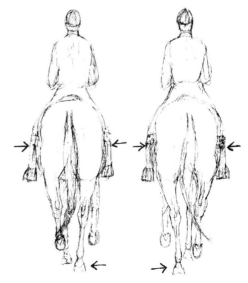

The driving aids for walk: push alternately with each leg, thus acting on each hind foot as it leaves the ground.

The driving aids for trot: push with both legs simultaneously, at the point when each hind foot is leaving the ground.

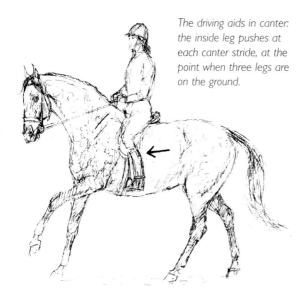

The driving aids in canter: the inside leg pushes at each canter stride, at the point when three legs are on the ground.

In **canter,** the inside leg pushes at each canter stride, at the point when three legs are on the ground. The other leg is held against the horse one hand's width further back, and controls the quarters.

2. Method of learning

• Concentrate on your body awareness, and focus your attention in particular on your hands, the supple coordination of your pelvis and thighs, and your lower legs, which should be in the basic position.

• Practise combining and coordinating the aids and using them in varying intensities, and at the same time try to refine them more and more.

• If you want to increase the strides, feel your hands yielding, your legs giving the forward-driving aids and your seat pushing forward in the saddle. If you want to make a downward transition or decrease the strides, feel your legs and seat pushing the horse forward while your hands stay put.

• What you are experiencing is the basic response: pushing and yielding serves to send the horse forwards, and pushing without yielding serves to slow the horse down or 'bring him back'.

• Pushing with alternate legs in time with the rhythm of the walk is best learned by letting your legs hang down limply and loosely. You will feel how

To start with, you can glance down to check that you are pushing correctly in walk.

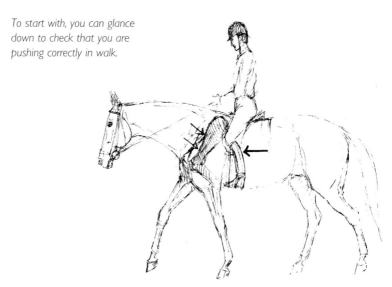

each leg comes momentarily against the horse's body and is then pushed off again. This is the exact rhythm in which, depending on the circumstances, your legs should either accompany the strides or push actively.

• To start with, check your feel for the correct driving aids in walk by glancing down: you are doing it correctly when your leg aid coincides with the point when the horse's shoulder on the same side is in its most rearward position.

• In sitting trot too, the best way to familiarise yourself with the feeling of the legs moving, and then pushing, rhythmically and elastically in time with the strides, is at first to let them hang down and go with the horse's movement, while you concentrate on what you are feeling.

• Sending the horse forward in rising trot is not difficult to learn, because it is easy to feel how your legs react when you sit down: it feels as if you are pressing them against the horse's body. You simply adjust this pressure in accordance with horse's responses.

• The aids for strike-off into canter, and synchronising the driving aids with the canter rhythm, are best picked up on the lunge. Focus on your body awareness: feel yourself moving from the hips with the horse's strides; feel how your inside leg comes against the horse's body at every canter stride, and focus on what you feel with your

To send the horse forward in rising trot, push as you you sit down (centre picture) – check that you have a light, even contact with the horse's mouth. (Photographed in Germany: for safety's sake a hard hat should be worn.)

In rising trot, press your legs against the horse's body as you sit down.

outside leg just after this. The best way to obtain a strike-off into canter is to replicate the feeling you experience at every canter stride.

• Obviously, to gauge your development you need a good instructor who can test your feel for the use of the forward-driving aids. In walk, tell him when you are pushing ("Left, right"); in trot (rising and sitting) and canter, say "Now – now – now!" at the appropriate moment. Say the same things to yourself when you are working alone.

• Halt after a successful exercise, and reinforce it by going through it in your mind. Visualise exactly what you felt. Finally, ride the same movement again and try to replicate this feeling. Tell your instructor when you think it is right, so that he can check.

> **IMPORTANT** Tell yourself: Even when I am past the initial learning stage, I will keep on asking my instructor to check my 'feel' and my 'self talk'.

• Develop this 'feel' at home as well, as a mental exercise.

• Make use of a camcorder as a training aid whenever possible. Ask one of your friends to video you. You can watch the video at home, and check and refine your 'feel'.

3. Tips for solving any problems which may arise

PROBLEM

It takes all your energy to get the horse to go forward to walk or trot.

TIPS

• Try to appreciate that school horses used to teaching beginners need to be fairly thick-skinned – otherwise they would bolt every time the rider did something clumsy or tactless!

• Feel what your hands are doing when you are pushing with your legs. Maybe you are not yielding enough, or only doing so on one side.

• Focus on your legs: are you applying them briefly, and then repeating the pressure as necessary? Or are you clamping them against the horse, i.e. prolonging the pressure, and so causing the horse to tense up and hold back?

• If your horse is simply too 'dead' or lazy for you to be able to get him to go forward, ask your instructor if you should use the whip behind your leg to back up your leg aid. After doing this, you should repeat the leg aid without the whip. You should then find it more effective!

• If you are really not getting anywhere, ask your instructor to put you on another horse. If there is a good reason, and you ask him nicely, he will understand!

PROBLEM

The strike-offs (departs) into canter are defeating you – there is too much to think about.

TIP

• Have another lesson on the lunge. Forget about the transition into canter as such. Instead, concentrate on what you are experiencing with each part of your body (seat, hip joints, legs, hands) as you canter. Simply do the same as you do at every canter stride: this is the best 'aid' for the transition into canter!

PROBLEM

You are successful in getting the horse to trot or canter on, but then he keeps going back into walk or trot again by himself.

TIPS

• Feel whether you have a light, even contact in your hands, or whether you are using them with a backward action or to hold on with. A quarter of an hour on the lunge can be beneficial, even for more experienced riders. Lunge lessons are by no means just for beginners! Remember: you can only apply the aids correctly if you have a supple, correct seat. It is worth taking the trouble to get it right from the beginning.

• Focus on your legs, and ensure that you are pushing in the right rhythm by talking yourself through the exercise in your head.

• Focus also on the combination of your pelvis and thighs: are you sitting

Lunge lessons are definitely not 'just for beginners'.

smoothly into the movement, or are you restricting or 'blocking' it, or sitting against it?

TELL YOURSELF I will have a lunge lesson before my faults develop into habits which will later be very difficult, if not impossible, to eradicate.

4. Suggestions for the instructor

• It is a good idea to encourage the student to discover for himself the feeling of pushing in time with each gait when needing more forward motion. Guide him by asking him to focus his awareness on the appropriate parts of his body.

• Next, give him time – he has plenty to keep him busy. Let him tell you when he thinks he has found the correct rhythm. Only if he cannot find the rhythm by himself should you help him by 'calling' it out for him.

• When the student finds the correct rhythm tell him so immediately. Ask him to halt and do an 'instant replay' in his mind. Again, give him time. Get him to tell you when he has managed to replicate the feeling exactly in his head.

• Next, ask him to ride the exercise again, and to tell you whether it feels the same as his mental rehearsal. Finally, ask him to call out to you when he is pushing, by saying "Left, right" in walk and "Now, now, now" in trot and canter.

• Between lessons encourage him to go over in his mind the impressions he has received, and next time you see him, ask him about his 'homework'.

5.2 THE HALF TURN ON THE FOREHAND

I. Aim

Description
In the half turn on the forehand the horse's hindlegs step 180° degrees around the forelegs. During the exercise the horse is flexed to the side of the rider's sideways-pushing leg.

Aids
The inside leg pushes sideways, and the rider places more weight on the inner half of the seat ('inner' and 'inside' always refers to the side to which the horse is flexed). After every two steps by the hindlegs (i.e. one complete stride), the rider 'catches up' the sideways movement with the outside leg and outside rein. The inside rein maintains the flexion. After a brief pause the aids are repeated until the half-turn is complete.

Uses
For the rider: It teaches the rider to use the sideways-pushing aids (inside leg) in conjunction with the regulating rein aids (diagonal aids). It provides a foundation for subsequent work entailing bends and flexions, namely

When riding a turn on the forehand, go onto an inside track before beginning the turn.

circles, turns and all lateral work.

For the horse: The turn on the forehand is a loosening exercise, and serves to introduce the young horse to the lateral aids (rein and leg active on the same side), or to remind an older horse of them.

Preconditions

For the rider: The rider must have mastered the coordination of the driving and restraining aids in all three basic paces.

For the horse: The horse should at least be thoroughly acquainted with the leg and rein aids in forward movement in the three basic paces. He must also have learned to stand still.

Preparation

Before the turn, bring the horse onto the inside track (about 80 cm/2ft 6in. in from the outside track), so that there is room for the head and neck to turn. Then flex the horse and move your outside leg a hand's breadth further

back. The inside leg remains in the normal position, with the rider's shoulder, hip and heel in line vertically.

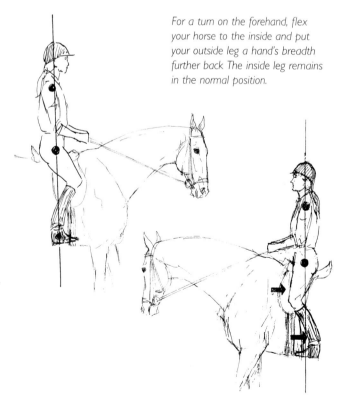

For a turn on the forehand, flex your horse to the inside and put your outside leg a hand's breadth further back The inside leg remains in the normal position.

2. Method of learning

• When your instructor has declared you ready to be introduced to the aids for the turn on the forehand, treat yourself to the luxury of a private lesson. You will be laying the foundations for numerous exercises which lie ahead, and which require the use of diagonal aids (inside leg – outside rein).

• Ask your instructor during this private lesson to ride the movement for you first. This will serve to retune the horse (which may have become rather lax) to the correct responses, i.e. to sensitive, unobtrusive aids. You can then be sure that the 'feel' you are getting is the right one.

NOTE New behaviour patterns, such as the application of the aids in the turn on the forehand, are much easier to learn correctly from the start than they are to put right later on.

• Watch the movement carefully, and picture it in your mind in detail, just as if you have already ridden it. Then sit on the horse and check by 'feel' that your legs are in the correct position. Your lower legs should be lightly touching the horse.

• You are now ready for your first attempt. Press with your inside leg, and let the horse take two steps (i.e. a

When riding a turn on the forehand, you could use use an abbreviated formula such as: "Inside (feel the step), regulate outside (outside rein and leg)".

complete stride) to the side. Then make a half-halt on the outside rein by asking and yielding, and 'let the horse feel' your outside leg. Repeat these steps until the turn is complete.

• Talk yourself through this as follows: "Inside (leg on) – step – leg off (inside), outside rein a bit stronger, and feel horse with outside leg". Shortened form: "Inside (feel the step), regulate outside (outside rein and leg)".

• To develop your 'feel', ask your instructor to tell you straight away when you get it right, so that you can do an exact 'action replay' in your mind (with eyes open or closed) in order to reinforce the lesson. At the second attempt, compare what you experience with what you felt the first time. Tell your instructor whether it felt the same or different. In this way, what you have learned becomes more and more established, until you have finally mastered the exercise. Tell your instructor again what it should feel like if ridden correctly, so that he can tell you if you are right.

• You can rehearse the turn on the forehand at home, in your mind, visualising the experience exactly as your instructor taught it to you.

• Also ask your instructor to adapt your verbal cues to prevent any faults from developing, for example: "inner knee low" if you feel that your weight is sliding to the outside.

• Keep asking your instructor to test you – this is not just something you do at the beginning. Remember that faults very quickly become established, and it is much easier to 'nip them in the bud'.

IMPORTANT Tell yourself: I must make a point of asking my instructor to help me in this way, even if I am not used to doing this. Any good instructor will find this acceptable, or even be pleased. Riding lessons are expensive: if I am not satisfied, I must change my instructor if necessary.

3. Tips for solving any problems which may arise

PROBLEM

The horse is not obeying the inside leg; he is not stepping sideways.

TIPS

• Back up the action of the inside leg with the whip by using the whip just behind it. Then apply the leg again, gently, without the whip. Impress on your mind exactly what you feel.

• Check the flexion. Check what you feel as you correct the flexion.

PROBLEM

Your horse goes sideways too fast, running away from the inside leg.

TIPS

• Remember to take your leg off again after applying it - do not keep on pressing or squeezing. Impress on your mind the following formula: "Press, step, yield". After a successful attempt, go over the experience in your mind to reinforce your memory of it.

• After every two steps by the hindfeet, let the horse feel your outside leg and outside rein. In this way you 'catch the horse up' with your outside (regulating) aids, and also build a slight pause into the movement.

PROBLEM

Your horse steps forwards.

TIPS

• When you first start riding the turn on the forehand it is acceptable for the horse to walk small circle with his forefeet.

• Focus on your outside hand, and perform a half-halt on the outside rein by asking and yielding.

• Focus on your outside leg, which should be regulating or 'limiting' the movement. If it is pressing in time with the inside leg, it is driving the horse forward.

IMPORTANT Tell yourself: I will remember every improvement and get it to 'gel' by reconstructing it in my mind afterwards, and then riding the movement again. I will ask my instructor to check that my feel is right: I will say "better" or "right" as appropriate, and he can compare this with what he sees.

4. Suggestions for the instructor

• Explain to the student precisely and patiently what he should do.

• Use demonstration material to enable the rider to visualise the movement - for example, get him to watch a turn on the forehand, either by riding it yourself or by showing him a video of it.

• Make sure that, to start with, he rides the exercise slowly and deliberately, that he stops after every two steps, and that he 'replays' the experience in his mind afterwards – get him to close his eyes if this will help.

• Ask him to say so out loud when he feels he has ridden the exercise correctly.

• Work out with him a formula for talking himself through it, and then reduce this to a shortened form (see above).

INSTRUCTOR'S TIP

Tell yourself: Even in a relatively simple exercise such as the turn on the forehand, I must place special emphasis on getting the rider to experience the movement precisely and in such a way that he can reproduce it. In this way I am laying important foundations for subsequent exercises.

5.3 LEG-YIELDING

I. Aim

Description

The horse moves at an angle of 45° to the track. He is flexed – not bent – in the direction of the sideways-pushing leg. His inside hind foot steps forward and across the outside one. In the easiest form of leg-yield the horse's head points towards the wall, which forms a barrier in front.

In the somewhat more difficult form, the horse's head points inwards. At a later stage, leg-yielding can also be ridden on a circle (on the half of the circle which does not touch the sides of the school), and from line to line (away from and back to the track).

Aids

With the legs in the position described for the walk, use your legs alternately in time with the movement, but ensure that the action of the inside leg predominates, so that the horse moves away from it. 'Catch the horse up' with your outside rein, thus preventing the shoulder from falling out. The outside leg limits the sideways displacement of the hindquarters into the school, so that the angle does not exceed 45° The outside leg also works with the inside leg to maintain the forward element of the movement. The rider's weight is placed slightly to the inside.

Uses

For the rider: Leg-yielding teaches the rider the use of the sideways-pushing leg in conjunction with that of the outside rein. Hence it is the next stage in the teaching of the diagonal aids, the easiest form of which was learned in the turn on the forehand.

For the horse: Leg-yielding is a good loosening exercise. It is also an effective means of teaching the young horse to respond to the sideways-pushing leg in forward movement, or to refine this response. When retraining spoiled horses, this exercise serves to

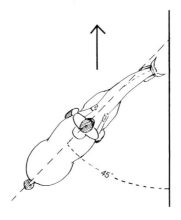

In the easiest form of leg-yielding, the horse's head points towards the wall.

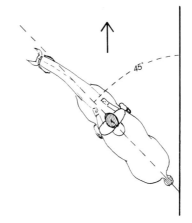

In this somewhat more difficult form of leg-yielding, the horse's head points towards the inside of the school.

Leg-yielding can also be performed on the open half of the circle which does not touch the sides of the school.

Leg-yielding can be ridden away from and back to the track (from line to line).

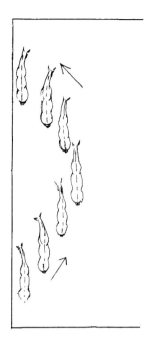

refamiliarise the horse with the correct response.

Preconditions

For the rider: You should have mastered the use and co-ordination of the diagonal aids (inside leg/outside rein) in the turn on the forehand, and have practised the following preparatory exercise: ride along the short side of the school on the outside track, and shortly before reaching the corner, flex your horse to the outside (towards the wall), leave your inside leg in the normal position (see above), and position your outside leg a hand's

In forward movement, push the hindquarters inwards off the track of the short side until the horse's longitudinal axis is at a maximum angle of 45° to the track.

breadth further back (see above). Then, still moving forward, push the hindquarters off the track into the school until the horse's body is at a maximum angle of 45° from the track. **For the horse:** He must have been taught the diagonal aids in the turn on the forehand, and be responsive to them.

2. Method of learning

• You will have studied and mentally rehearsed the new exercise as often and precisely as possible beforehand.

• Treat yourself to another private lesson for the purposes of learning this exercise.

• As with learning all new exercises, it is very helpful if your instructor rides the horse briefly beforehand. Ask him to demonstrate the movement to you during your private lesson – this will give you another chance to see it. Moreover, your horse may have become rather lax, and this will serve to retune him to the correct aids, and sharpen up his responses. You can then be sure that he is giving you the correct feel for the movement.

IMPORTANT Tell yourself: I can only learn effectively if my horse responds accurately to correct, light aids.

USEFUL TIP Especially when learning new exercises, private lessons are highly beneficial, and in the long run they pay for themselves.

• Leg-yielding can be rehearsed again mentally at home, when it should feel exactly as your instructor taught it to you.

• A good preliminary exercise is the **turn about the forehand in motion** (in Germany this is called the **swinging volte**). You can start with the turn on the forehand, with which you are already familiar. To give yourself the necessary space for this exercise, go into the centre of a circle. Begin the turn on the forehand, and then with the outside rein, while moving forward, lead the forehand sideways until you are in the 'swinging volte'. Hence this is basically a turn on the forehand in slow forward/sideways movement.

• When you have mastered this exercise, ride the leg-yielding exercise from the short side to the long side, as described above.

• With your instructor work out a

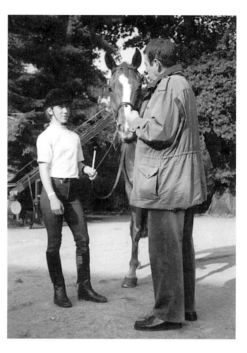

Discuss your 'self talk' with your instructor.

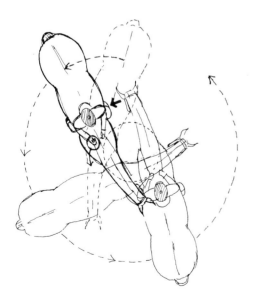

The turn about the forehand in motion, or 'swinging volte'.

formula that you can use to help you. It might go something like: "Inside strongly (leg), outside gently (feel), contain with outside rein (by asking and yielding)". If problems arise, your instructor can change the formula, e.g. "(with the) inside hand (maintain the) flexion".

• **Developing your feel:** Ask your instructor to tell you immediately when the ratio of forward to sideways movement is correct. Then halt and do an 'instant replay' in your mind of the exact feeling you experienced. Finally, ride the exercise again and try to reproduce this feeling. Tell your instructor when you think you have got it right, so that he can judge.

• Do not be afraid to keep asking your instructor on an on-going basis to check you out when you feel you are doing it correctly, and to monitor your 'self talk'.

3. Tips for solving any problems which arise

PROBLEM

Your horse does not move away easily enough from the inside leg.

TIPS

• Check you are ready to go on to this stage by reviewing the turn on the forehand.

• Before you begin, feel your legs pushing alternately, and in the same rhythm apply the formula: "Inside strongly – outside gently". Your action will then be correct, as you will be acting on the hind foot which is leaving the ground.

• Use your whip briefly behind your leg to back up your leg aid. Then repeat the leg pressure more gently and without the whip. Impress on your mind exactly what it feels like.

Feel your legs pushing alternately: 'Inside strongly – outside gently'.

PROBLEM

The horse falls out onto his shoulder and escapes sideways with too much bend in his neck.

Too much bend in the neck, shoulder falling out and escaping sideways.

TIPS

• Focus on your outside hand, keep a steady contact with the horse's mouth and limit or regulate the bend by gently opening and closing your fingers.

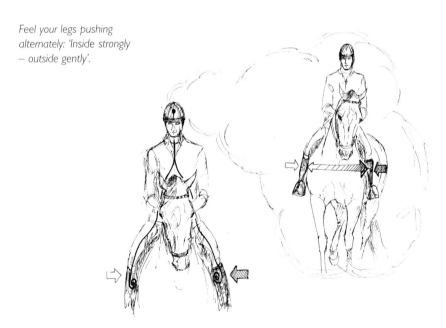

• Straighten the neck, and ride forward a short distance in a straight position before beginning the leg-yield again.

PROBLEM

Your horse is not going forwards sufficiently, and is not stepping rhythmically with one hind foot over the other.

TIPS

• Feel how much pressure you have in your hands, and make a point of reducing it.

• Focus on the alternating action of your legs.

• Look round at the hindquarters and check that what you feel is the correct angle has not, in fact, been exceeded.

> **CAUTION** Tell yourself: In the leg-yield, my horse must have enough room to cross the inside leg over the outside one without treading on his opposite coronet. Hence the angle should not be greater than 45°.

4. Suggestions for the instructor

• As with the turn on the forehand, start by using demonstration material and explanations to create an exact picture of the movement in the student's mind.

• Refer back to the turn on the forehand, with which the student is already familiar, and explain to him which aids and movements the two exercises have in common, and which

Check that the angle is not greater than 45°.

are the ones he will meet for the first time in the leg-yield.

• In particular, create in his mind an image of the forward movement and the correct angle.

• Ask for only a few steps sideways to begin with. When you have managed to obtain these, ask the student to halt, do an 'instant replay' of what he experienced, and then ride the movement again. Let him tell you himself how it felt the next time.

• If after several attempts you have had no success, get on the horse yourself and demonstrate the movement. This has two advantages: you are showing him the exercise, and at the same time you are sharpening up the horse's responses to the aids, thus making it easier for the student to feel how to give the aids correctly.

• If you are having problems with the

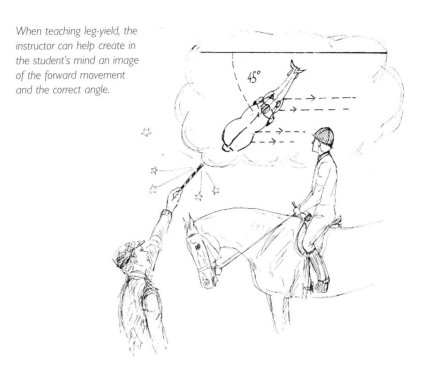

When teaching leg-yield, the instructor can help create in the student's mind an image of the forward movement and the correct angle.

45°

rein aids, take hold of the reins behind the bit rings to convey to the rider what he should feel.

> **REMEMBER**   Only on a responsive, 'finely-tuned' horse can the student gain and assimilate a feel for the correct aids.

5.4   RIDING TURNS, CIRCLES AND CURVES

I. Aim

Description and aids
Before you start a simple **turn**, flex your horse to the side to which you wish to turn. How long beforehand you need to do this depends on how long it will take you to flex the horse and make him light on the inside rein.

To ride the turn, guide ('lead') the horse with the inside rein into the new direction, then yield. Put more weight onto the inside half of your seat (or, in rising trot, onto the inside stirrup), and 'feel' the horse with the inside leg.

At the same time, use an outside, regulating rein aid to prevent him falling out onto his outside shoulder. The outside leg, one hand's breadth behind the basic position, 'contains' the turn, by ensuring that the hind feet remain on the same track as the fore feet and do not step outwards.

Turns vary in difficulty. The easiest is a turn of only a few degrees, as found for example in the change of rein across the diagonal. The degree of difficulty increases as the figures themselves become progressively more difficult (see illustrations on following pages).

A **circle** is the continuation of a turn. At a later stage, the horse's whole body should be bent onto the line being ridden. In other words, the longitudinal axis should correspond with the track to be followed.

Here again there are different degrees of difficulty, ranging from the largest diameter circle to the smallest, tightest circle, which is the 5-metre circle or volte. Between these extremes are a multitude of different curved tracks: the tighter the bend, the more difficult they are. For example, riding two shallow loops in from the track is more difficult than riding one with a single loop. Likewise, a 10-metre circle is easier than a volte, and is found in dressage tests of a lower level.

Corners are also examples of circular or curved tracks. When you ride a corner correctly, you describe a quarter of a circle or volte (ranging from 10 metres in diameter down to the minimum size of 5 metres). You will not manage this straight away, but you can at least round the corners – there is not much point in riding the horse through the corners in an unbent, straight position! To start with, join up the two corners of the short side to make a single, large-diameter curved

To ride a turn, guide the horse into the new direction with the inside rein, and then yield. In rising trot, place more weight on the inside stirrup and 'feel' the horse with the inside leg.

track, i.e. half of a 20-metre circle, and try to bend your horse accordingly.

You should ride corners this way if:

a) this is the maximum bend your horse can manage as yet; or

b) you yourself have not yet learned the technique for bending the horse.

It is important that you start off by practising the technique of flexing and

Use outside regulating leg and rein aids to prevent the horse falling out onto his outside shoulder.

Changing the rein (direction) across the diagonal.

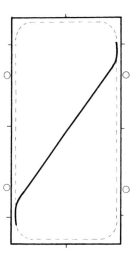

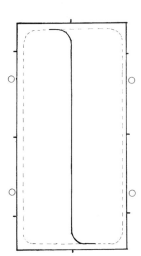

Changing the rein (direction) down the centre of the school.

Diagonal change of rein (direction) to the half-marker.

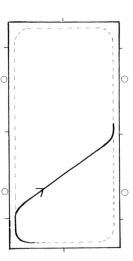

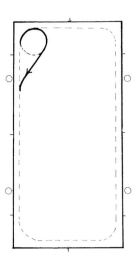

Changing the rein (direction) through half a 5-metre circle or volte in the corner.

bending on a gentle curve, and become thoroughly familiar with the correct feel. With time, you will gradually learn to bend the horse to tighter curves.

Riding large diameter curved tracks is of fundamental importance in learning to bend the horse, and is also an excellent loosening exercise for him. On a circle in trot and canter, hollow the horse on the inside of the circle, and stretch him on the outside. Maintain the

bend with the inside leg. Check the result by pushing your inside hand forward (10-20 cm/4-8in.): if the bend is correct, the horse will maintain the flexion of his own accord.

The inside leg, at the girth, has a sideways-pushing action, while the outside 'regulating' leg is positioned a hand's breadth further back. The outside rein backs up the action of the outside leg: by maintaining a steady contact with the horse's mouth it

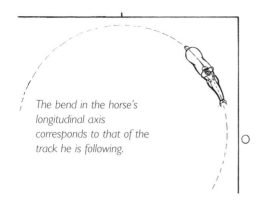

The bend in the horse's longitudinal axis corresponds to that of the track he is following.

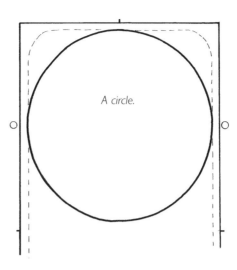

A circle.

prevents excessive longitudinal bend, while at the same time allowing the necessary stretching of the outside of the horse.

Hence the outside leg and outside rein work in unison in a regulating capacity, while the inside hand, by asking and yielding, assists the inside leg in obtaining the flexion and bend, making the horse hollow on the inside of the circle.

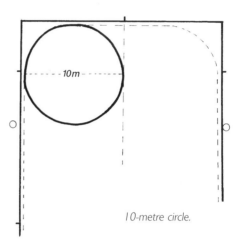

10-metre circle.

IMPORTANT At the **FIRST SIGN OF LOSS OF IMPULSION,** however slight, immediately **RIDE YOUR HORSE FORWARD AGAIN ON A STRAIGHT LINE**.

Go back onto the circle only when the impulsion has been restored. Change the rein frequently (approximately every five minutes), even if the flexion and bend on one rein are unsatisfactory. Have the utmost patience with yourself and your horse. If you only succeed in part, at least you know you are on the right track, and have succeeded in laying the foundations for good, gymnastic training.

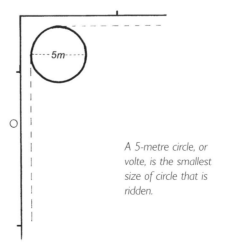

A 5-metre circle, or volte, is the smallest size of circle that is ridden.

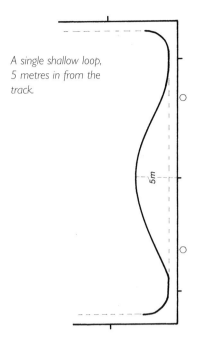

A single shallow loop, 5 metres in from the track.

5m

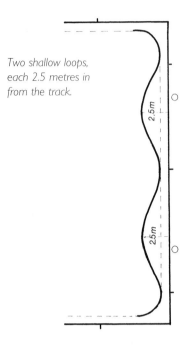

Two shallow loops, each 2.5 metres in from the track.

2.5m

2.5m

Uses

For the rider: This work develops and refines your technique in using the diagonal aids (see turn on the forehand, and leg-yielding), and teaches you to use them in movement to bend the horse. Thus you learn to make your horse more supple and connected, or 'through', and so improve him.

For the horse: Bending work also benefits the straightness. The horse learns to step forwards under his centre of gravity with his hindlegs (instead of stepping out to one side, being 'crooked'). Only if this foundation has been laid can the more advanced exercises in collection and extension be meaningfully performed. (See also

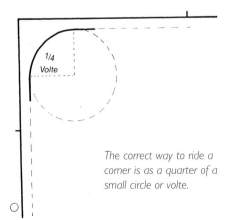

1/4
Volte

The correct way to ride a corner is as a quarter of a small circle or volte.

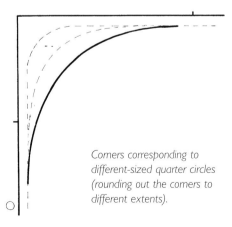

Corners corresponding to different-sized quarter circles (rounding out the corners to different extents).

'Dressage Tips and Training Solutions' by P. and W. Hölzel, and M. Plewa, published by Kenilworth Press in the UK and Trafalgar Square in the USA.)

Preconditions

For the rider: You must have mastered the use of the diagonal aids in the turn on the forehand and the leg-yield.

For the horse: Your horse must have learned to bend on large diameter circular tracks in response to the use of the sideways-pushing leg.

2. Method of learning

• In order to learn to ride turns and circular tracks, it is particularly important that you start off by forming an exact picture in your mind of what you are planning to learn. Do this by watching the movements being performed and looking at appropriate visual aids, such as books, drawings, films and videos.

• Rehearse the turning and circling exercises mentally, even before you start trying to ride them.

• Ask your instructor to take hold of the reins behind the bit rings to convey to you the feeling of slowly asking and giving with the inside rein while maintaining a contact on the outside rein.

• Afterwards, impress on your memory through mental rehearsal what you felt on each rein.

• If this memory fades after a few lessons, ask your instructor to renew it for you.

• Start by performing, in walk and trot, a turn of only a few degrees, as found

for example in the change of rein across the diagonal.

• When your instructor gives the command to turn, if you have a horse in front of you, try to turn slightly before the other rider so that your horse doesn't simply follow the horse in front.

• Each time you turn, focus on your body, and what you are doing with your hands, weight and legs.

• Keep practising the finely balanced synchronisation of the aids, in their different gradations and nuances.

• Tell your instructor the formula you are using. This might be, for example: "Inside (hand, weight, leg), outside (hand, leg)".

• When riding a corner, i.e. performing a quarter-circle, your formula should be approximately as follows: "Flexion, bend (inside leg), lighter (inside hand half way through the corner), straighten (coming out of the corner)".

• Even when you are past the initial stage, ask your instructor to keep monitoring your 'feel' and your 'self talk'.

IMPORTANT   Tell yourself: I will also mentally practise using and co-ordinating many different combinations of aids. I can do this off the horse, for example, in the stable, while watching someone else riding, or at home.

• Make use of a camcorder at every opportunity. Ask a friend to video you. Watch the video in peace at home, and monitor and refine your body awareness. Also remember your instructor's corrections and comments in respect of each individual exercise.

3. Tips for solving any problems which may arise

PROBLEM

Your horse is not accepting the inside rein, and is leaning on your inside hand.

TIPS

• Make sure that when you ask with your inside hand, you yield again immediately and are not pulling.

• Give several small half-halts rather than one big one.

• Flex your horse briefly to the inside sometimes while riding straight ahead down the long side of the school.

• Practise flexing the horse (laterally) in halt, like you do when preparing to perform a turn on the forehand.

• Pause immediately after a successful attempt, and commit to memory what you have just experienced.

• Ask your instructor to let you feel through the reins how much you should ask and yield with your hands.

PROBLEM

Your horse falls out through the outside shoulder.

TIPS

• Check your outside hand. It should be controlling the outside of the horse,

and should therefore be maintaining a contact with the mouth.

• Check that your outside leg is in a 'regulating' position, about a hand's breadth behind the basic position.

• Revise the regulating function of the outside leg and rein by riding the turn on the forehand.

• You can also practise this in the leg-yield, either along the long side of the school, or on the part of a circle which is away from the sides of the school.

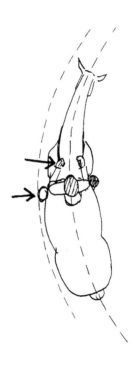

Correcting a horse that falls out through the outside shoulder.

PROBLEM

Your horse responds to the inside leg either insufficiently or not at all.

TIPS

• Retune him to the inside leg in the turn on the forehand and/or leg-yield.

• If your horse does not respond, you can reinforce the action of your leg by using the whip just behind it.

• Ask your instructor to retune your horse, and to get him to respond to subtle aids.

• After a successful attempt, and when you are no longer on the horse, run through the experience again, in your mind.

TELL YOURSELF Since learning to flex and bend the horse is so important for the rest of my equestrian education, I must be correct in every detail.

4. Suggestions for the instructor

• The best way to convey the feeling of the inside rein slowly asking and yielding while the outside rein maintains a contact, is to take hold of the reins behind the bit rings and ask the student to feel how the aids should be applied.

• Begin with single, large diameter turns, and take special care to ensure that the student acquires the right feel for the flexion and bend. The correctness of the school figures can wait!

• If the student is experiencing difficulties, for example, with his inside leg aid, go back to simpler exercises (turn on the forehand, leg-yielding).

• You will make it easier for him to learn the correct aids if you fine-tune his horse so that he can feel exactly how he should apply the aids.

• Be generous with the praise when the exercise has been done correctly, and ask the student to do an exact replay in his mind in order to commit the experience to memory and enable him to repeat it.

INSTRUCTOR'S TIP

TAKE YOUR TIME. By conveying to the student and impressing on his mind how to flex and bend the horse correctly on turns and circular tracks, you are laying important foundations for much of his subsequent training.

• In a private lesson if necessary, ride the student's horse for him on a circle, with the correct flexion and bend, so that he can visualise exactly what he is trying to achieve. The horse may have become rather lazy, so retune him so that he will respond to correct, subtle aids, and so give the rider the correct feel for the exercise.

INSTRUCTOR'S TIP

IMPORTANT Tell yourself: Only if I enable the student to get exactly the right feel will he make reliable progress.

5.5   REIN-BACK

I. Aim

Description
The horse should step backwards in a diagonal sequence, while remaining on the bit and letting the aids through; he should not show resistance. In order to

Diagonal sequence of steps in the rein-back.

finish with the horse standing square, end the exercise with a half step.

Aids

Begin the movement by giving the same aids as for moving forwards from halt, but instead of yielding with the hands, softly 'catch' and restrain the forward movement. You should then feel the horse yield in his mouth to the contact. Immediately after the first step backwards, lighten your hands and become passive in your seat. Repeat these aids, lightly, at every step.

Uses

For the rider: You learn greater discernment and refinement in the

You begin the rein-back with the same aids as for moving forward from halt, except that you do not yield with your hands.

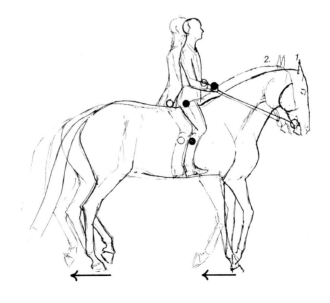

Horse standing square.

synchronised use of the aids.

You are also learning an early form of the aids you will use later to shorten or collect the horse in forward movement.

For the horse: This is a good gymnastic exercise, and especially useful for increasing the engagement of the hindquarters, and bending the hip and stifle joints. It also helps to make the horse more connected or 'through'.

Preconditions

For the rider: You must have learned the coordination of the aids through doing half-halts and downward transitions, e.g. transitions from canter to trot, from trot to walk, and from walk or trot to halt.

For the horse: He should be on the aids, at least enough for him to be able to make a transition softly from canter, down through trot and walk, to halt. He should have learned to increase and decrease the strides in trot, and to stand square and on the bit in halt.

2. Method of learning

• With this exercise, you can only learn through watching if the aids are explained to you at the same time. The most common fault lies in the rider's hands: if they start off by acting in a backwards direction, then it is best that you do not watch that particular rider – you will be learning the wrong aids!

• Picture exactly a forward transition from halt, but with your hands staying put instead of yielding. Just before your horse yields to the contact and steps back, the contact feels stronger. This is because you are pushing the horse into it: it should never be due to a backward movement of the hands.

WHAT TO LOOK OUT FOR

Say to yourself: Just before I make my hands lighter, I will feel an increase in pressure on my ring finger, resulting from pushing the horse forward, and not from drawing my hands back!

• Lay special emphasis on learning the rein-back correctly from the start. In this exercise, faults which arise at the beginning in the application of the aids are particularly detrimental and difficult to eradicate.

• For this reason, you would do well to treat yourself to another private lesson for the purpose of learning this exercise.

• It is a big help if your horse has been 'retuned' by your instructor beforehand so that he responds to correct, subtle aids. This is the best and most direct way to ensure that you experience the right feel.

Prior to the rein-back, your horse should be halted, 'round', light and on the bit.

• Begin the rein-back only when your horse is halted, 'round', on the bit and light on the contact. (Your instructor can guide you here if you are not sure.) If the horse does not meet these criteria, reining back is out of the question; it simply will not work!

• To start with, practise only the first stage of the rein-back. Feel your legs driving the horse and your seat pushing elastically forward in the saddle. This action causes you to experience a temporary increase in pressure on each ring finger. If your horse steps backwards, feel your contact with the horse's mouth become lighter, along with your driving aids.

• If, in the early stages, your horse steps forwards, you are on the right track: you have simply yielded with your hands instead of keeping them in the same position.

• **Training your 'feel'**: Here also it is crucial to the learning process that your instructor acknowledges the first signs of success. Ask him to help you with this. As with the other exercises, review the experience intensively in your mind afterwards, and then ride the exercise again with your instructor monitoring you.

• Discuss with your instructor your verbal cues. The following, for example, might be helpful: "Forwards (push), hands (feel the pressure), lighter (all aids)".

• Next, at each step backwards, perform a refined version of what you have learned.

• Ask your instructor to keep monitoring your 'feel' and your accompanying verbal cues. This is not something you do only at the beginning.

HELPFUL TIP Practise the first stage often, so as to acquire the right feel for the synchronisation of the aids. Never ask for too much too soon (several steps in a row), and in so doing resort to pulling.

3. Tips for solving any problems which may arise

PROBLEM

Your horse is resisting by throwing his head up and refusing to go backwards.

TIPS

• Stop, and go back and fulfil the requirements for starting this exercise - the horse must be 'round' and on the bit in the halt.

• To achieve this, first ride forwards; do not attempt to get your horse on the bit in halt straightaway, or even in walk; use an energetic forward gait, preferably trot. Make sure that your horse performs the transitions to halt correctly, and remains 'round' and light in the hand.

• At the beginning of the exercise, focus your attention on the ring finger of each hand. At the same time, monitor what you are doing with your hands.

• Also focus on your legs and seat. Check that you are not using them excessively or abruptly.

• Practise obtaining frequent, good, entries into rein-back.

• As a temporary measure, you can ride your horse a bit deeper (with a longer and lower head carriage) beforehand.

• Check that the horse is on the aids by performing transitions, and by increasing and decreasing the strides.

If you have difficulties with the rein-back, it may help to ride your horse a bit deeper (with a longer and lower head carriage) beforehand.

PROBLEM

The horse goes sideways, usually to the right.

TIPS

• Check that the light pressure you feel in your hands at the beginning is the same on each side, and that you are not drawing one hand back behind the other.

• Position the leg slightly further back on the side towards which the horse is stepping, and use it a bit more actively than the other leg, so as to limit the sideways movement.

PROBLEM

The horse takes more steps backwards than required.

• Keep varying the number of steps you ask for.

• Make frequent transitions from the rein-back into forward movement, such as into walk.

4. Instructor's tip from author's experience

A talented student of mine was preparing for a fairly advanced riding exam. However, she was experiencing considerable difficulty with the rein-back. She always used her hands first (and therefore backwards), and did not push the horse forwards with her legs until afterwards. Consequently, the horse was 'locking up' against the aids, scrambling awkwardly sideways, and coming above the bit.

I had already told her what she was doing wrong, but the results were still not satisfactory. So I decided that this time I would not refer directly to the old fault: instead I would build up a whole new picture of the movement in her mind.

I asked the rider to halt, explained the aids to her again, got her to rehearse these mentally, and together we worked out a verbal formula to use: "Legs and weight (as in a forward transition), hand (stays put), lighter (all the aids)". I told her: "If your horse steps forward first, you are on the right track. You have simply used your hand a bit late."

Her next attempt was better, but was still not good enough. I could see that the horse was not responding adequately. So I asked the student to dismount, and got on the horse and retuned it to the aids.

After I had done this, the student managed to do the first step impeccably. I asked her to halt, and got her to do an exact and intensive mental replay of what she had just experienced. Afterwards I asked her to ride forwards again, then halt; the three steps of rein-back which followed were flawless.

For 'homework' I asked her go over the movement again, and to recreate exactly in her mind the feeling she had experienced.

The next day, she was successful at the first attempt. She looked radiant. "That was exactly as I visualised it!", she said.

Dr Hölzel and a student discuss their work.

When she went on to ride the whole of the test containing the rein-back, and even, later, when she rode it in the exam, there were no further problems. We had got to the root of the problem! The exercise had become automatic.

Tell yourself: I will achieve far more by forming a whole new mental picture of the movement than by using faults as my starting point.

CHAPTER

6

JUMPING AND THE LIGHT OR HALF SEAT

6.1 RIDING IN THE LIGHT OR HALF SEAT

1. Aim

You use the light or half seat for fast work and for long distances, in order to reduce the strain on the horse's back as well as on your own. Hence you use it for cross-country riding, hunting, and jumping.

Shorten the stirrups by two to three holes than in the basic seat, to allow your knee to be firmer against the saddle. Your weight is carried on your knees and stirrups, with your seat out of the saddle slightly, and your upper body a little in front of the vertical. Your hands have an elastic contact with the horse's mouth, and are carried alongside the neck below the crest.

As the pace increases, you incline your upper body further forward, so as to keep your centre of gravity above that of the horse.

If you want to increase or decrease the pace, you bring your upper body back slightly, and bring your seat closer to, but not **into** the saddle. You do this, for example, before and after each jump, and before turning. To decrease the pace, you ride from your legs to your hands – the latter remain low, and are used with an asking and yielding action.

It is essential that you master the light or half seat if you want to go out hacking and riding across country – something which every rider looks forward to being able to do.

You are ready to start learning the light or half seat when you have mastered the basic seat in all three gaits.

2. Method of learning

• Before you start, closely study the use of this seat as often as you can, and create an image of it in your mind.

• Treat yourself to a private lesson as an introduction to the light or half seat.

• Ask your instructor to tell you

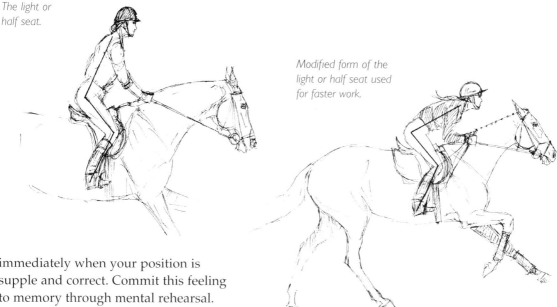

The light or half seat.

Modified form of the light or half seat used for faster work.

immediately when your position is supple and correct. Commit this feeling to memory through mental rehearsal. Then practise the position again, and try to replicate this feeling. Tell your instructor when you think you have achieved this, and ask him to monitor you.

• Later, while out on a ride, you can commit to memory the feel of the more forward form of the seat used for faster work.

• Ask your instructor to tell you, if he forgets, whether you are practising this modified form correctly.

• You will have no problem recalling, and therefore practising in your mind afterwards, the incomparable experience of a cross-country canter.

3. Suggestions for the instructor

• An effective way to teach the light or half seat is to practise it first in walk and then in trot. The rider 'remains standing'; he does not let his seat down into the saddle. He absorbs the

movement through his ankles, knees and hips.

• Riding over cavalletti is a good exercise which helps the rider find his balance and go with the movement.

• As usual, use mental rehearsal to reinforce the feel of the light or half seat in walk, trot and canter.

Riding over cavalletti.

Practising the light or half seat in trot.

• You can develop the rider's suppleness by getting him to alternate between sitting canter and canter in the light or half seat.

• Start off by training the feel for the 'faster' form of the jumping seat in the outside arena, and then reinforce it by mental rehearsal. Only then should the student be allowed to try it out for real on a ride.

6.2 JUMPING

1. Aims

Before you start jumping, you must be confirmed in the light seat, and have learned to accompany the horse's movements correctly over cavalletti. Jumping can be broken down into four distinct phases:

1. The approach
2. The take-off
3. The landing
4. The recovery and getaway

You **approach** the jump in the basic canter (a brisk working-to-medium canter), straight, and in the light or half seat. When the horse sees the jump, and so increases the pace slightly, you move your upper body forward accordingly. Your hands allow the neck to stretch, without abandoning the contact with the mouth.

On **take-off**, the upper body points straight ahead, bends from the hips, and accompanies the movement by going forwards and downwards, so that it forms an almost parallel line with the horse's back. The hands yield just enough for the horse to be able to stretch sufficiently, while still maintaining a contact. At the same time, the heels are pressed down to prevent the lower leg from sliding back.

You can only sit correctly **over the jump** if you sit and 'go with' the horse correctly during the take-off. If you notice that your hands are restricting the freedom of the horse's neck, push

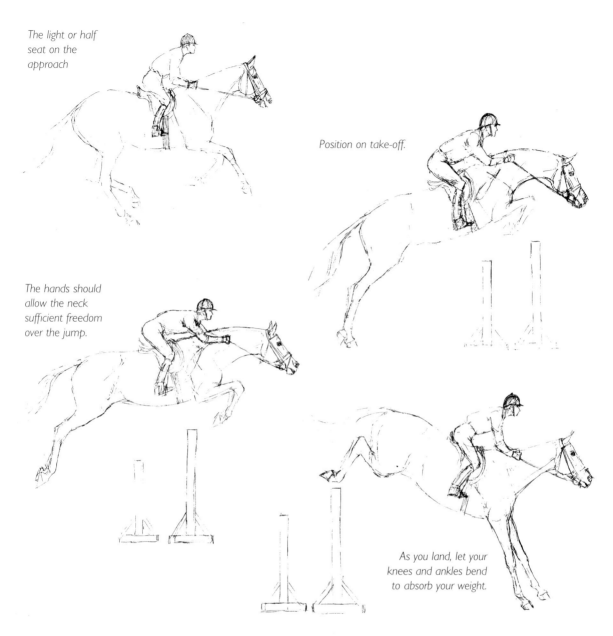

The light or half seat on the approach

Position on take-off.

The hands should allow the neck sufficient freedom over the jump.

As you land, let your knees and ankles bend to absorb your weight.

them forward immediately – it is better to have the reins 'on the long side' than too short!

During the **landing**, let your knees and ankles bend to absorb your weight, and as soon as all four of the horse's legs have touched down, bring your upper body back to the normal light or half seat position.

After the jump, ride in the basic jumping canter towards the next fence. If there are no more jumps, ride a transition down to trot, and then walk, but only when your horse is cantering under control and is light in the hand. If the horse speeds up after the jump, turn onto a circle to make it easier to bring him back to the basic pace, and onto the aids. In other words, do not stop until your horse is going in the same way as you would like him to go between jumps. If he lands with the wrong leg leading, or disunited, go back to trot before striking off in the correct canter (later you can use a flying change).

2. Method of learning

• When learning to jump, qualified instruction is especially important, first and foremost for the prevention of accidents and falls, which result in fear and loss of confidence. Never let yourself be persuaded by one of your friends to 'have a go' over a small jump when nobody qualified is around. This is simply dangerous and irresponsible.

Use pictures to impress on your mind what the jumping seat should look like. (Blyth Tait tackles a trakehner.)

• On the other hand, once the preparatory work has been completed and you satisfy all the requirements, there is nothing out of the ordinary or difficult about jumping. It is just something you learn to do, like everything else. And, as you will see, it can be a lot of fun! However, safety is paramount. Even when you have a bit of experience behind you, a hard hat is a 'must', and there is no place for recklessness or showing off.

REMEMBER Tell yourself: Qualified instruction is especially important for jumping. It will protect me and my horse from accidents.

• It may be that you are afraid to try jumping. Perhaps this is due to something which has happened to you, to someone else having a bad fall, or to something you have been told. You can eliminate this fear by carrying out the best possible preparation, taking all the necessary precautions, and by training your mind. If, having done this, you are still afraid, you should speak up and say so. Your instructor will take this into consideration. Never let yourself be persuaded to 'just close your eyes and go for it'! (See Chapter 2: "Coping with Fear".)

• Before your first jumping lesson, form an exact picture in your mind of all the phases of the jump by watching jumping lessons and videos, and put yourself mentally in the rider's place (ride with him in your mind).

• Do an exact 'action replay' in your mind of what you have seen.

• Keep practising the light or half seat on the flat. Use it while practising transitions from working canter to extended canter, and back again.

• Look upon the jump as a one big (long and high) canter stride. Simulate going with the horse on take-off; do this over and over again, at first with a qualified instructor, and then alone.

• Ask your instructor to convey to you what the basic canter used for jumping feels like.

• Also ask him to let you practise in halt or walk what is involved in 'going with' the horse on take-off. He should be only too pleased to grant your request to do preparatory exercises over cavalletti.

• When your instructor says you are 'going with' the horse correctly, and have mastered the basic canter, replay your experience in your mind, like a film. You can do this on the horse, say, during walk intervals or at the end of the lesson, or without the horse at home and elsewhere.

• During jumping training, ask your instructor to give you an assessment of your position and actions during each phase of the jump.

• Ask him to let you repeat the phase or phases which were not satisfactory.

• Immediately he gives his seal of approval, reinforce your experience by doing an 'instant replay' of it in your mind.

NOTE Tell yourself: If I do all the relevant forms of preparation and mental training, I will learn to jump just as certainly as I learned everything else.

3. Tips for dealing with any problems which may arise

PROBLEM

You are getting left behind, and either restricting the horse with your hands, or falling down onto his back.

TIPS

• Practise 'going with' the horse as an exercise in its own right, on the flat, and create a new mental image of it.

• Ask your instructor to monitor you as you talk through an intensive visualisation of a successful jump you have just done.

• Ask him to 'retune' your horse if you cannot control it, i.e. you cannot regulate the tempo.

PROBLEM

The horse runs away after the jump.

TIPS

• Turn onto a circle, get the horse under control, and come back to trot only when the canter is right.

• You might ask your instructor to let you ride another horse which is quieter and more controllable over jumps.

• Practise slowing the strides on the flat, using the light or half seat.

PROBLEM

Your horse slows down as he approaches the jump, and/or refuses.

TIPS

• Use the driving aids energetically in time with the canter rhythm.

• Use the whip on the horse's shoulder to back up the leg aids – apply the whip by turning your hand from the wrist, and take care not to pull the horse in the mouth as you do so.

• Check that you are approaching the jump straight, and ensure that you are yielding with your hands before and over the jump.

• Ask your instructor to ride the horse over the jump, to show you how to ride an effective approach, and at the same time to improve your horse's responses.

PROBLEM

Your horse starts to rush as he approaches the jump, and you are unable to regulate the pace.

TIPS

• Practise slowing the pace in the light or half seat on the flat.

• When slowing the pace, check that your hands are yielding immediately after the half-halt.

• Ask your instructor if you may turn away from the jump onto a circle immediately your horse starts to rush.

• Ask him to 'retune' your horse, or to let you ride another one.

SPEAK UP   Tell yourself: If I have given it my best shot, and am still getting nowhere, I will ask my instructor to get on the horse and 'retune' him, or give me another horse.

4. Suggestions for the instructor

• Always insist that an approved riding hat is worn.

• You must also ensure that, for your part, you do everything possible to avoid accidents.

• If the rider tells you he does not want to jump today, never talk him into doing it!

• Always end the lesson at the 'last but one jump'; in other words, at a point when the student is in a position to go on to do another, more difficult jump. This enables you to finish on a good note, and provides a sound basis for future training. This applies equally to both horse and rider.

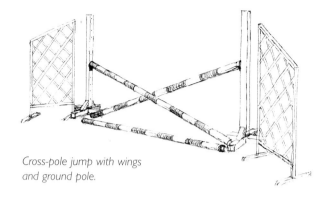

Cross-pole jump with wings and ground pole.

AS A BASIC PRINCIPLE Tell yourself: I will stop at the 'last jump but one'. This is in the interests of safety, and is also good for the rider's morale.

• For beginners in particular, nothing should be too much trouble. For example, cross-pole jumps encourage the horse to jump in the centre. You can also make the learning process easier by the use of wings, a take-off pole, and low cavalletti placed at trot and later canter distances in front of the jump.

• It goes without saying that the

beginner, in particular, should ride a well-trained jumper. What he could really do with is a horse which 'does it all by itself', as they say, and which has no vices, does not overreact, and jumps reliably and calmly.

• A good way to teach the take-off is as an exercise in its own right, on the flat, backed up by review and mental rehearsal of the rider's actions and experiences.

• A very good way to convey to the rider the yielding action of the hands

The instructor can convey to the student the feeling of yielding with his hands by taking hold of the reins just behind the bit rings.

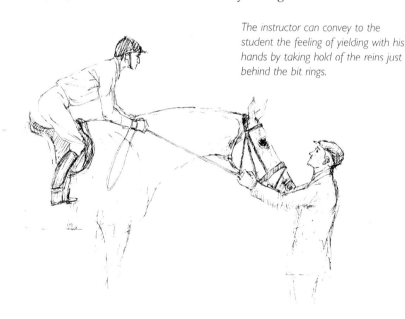

A placing pole or ground pole, one canter stride before the jump, makes it easier to take off at the right place.

during take-off, is to take hold of the reins just behind the bit rings and simulate the stretching movement of the horse's neck.

• A good thing to do while you are practising on the flat is to train the student to react promptly to cues. For example, 'one' = position of the upper body in the jumping seat; 'two' = seat on the approach; 'three' = seat during

take-off; and 'four' = seat during landing.

• When the student responds quickly enough to your voice during practice on the flat, you can do the same thing over the jumps, and you will find it a very effective training aid.

• Later, for the jumping from canter, abbreviate your voice commands to: "Push – push – and – now – forward",

Low grids of trotting or cantering poles are good for training the rider's seat over fences.

spoken clearly and in rhythm with the stride.

• A placing pole, one canter stride before the jump, makes it easier to take off at the right place, and helps the student to 'go with' the movement.

• To begin with, follow up and reinforce every achievement by getting the rider to go back over it in his mind, and then to repeat the process at home afterwards.

• The same goes for the teaching of the basic canter pace, first on the flat, then over the jumps.

• Having taught the student the correct feel in this way, test him by getting him to talk you through what he experienced.

• Low grids of trotting or cantering poles are an effective means of further developing and confirming the seat over fences.

INSTRUCTOR'S TIP

DIRECTIVE IDEA Tell yourself: when teaching a beginner-rider to jump, nothing should be left to chance. I am answerable for the rider's safety as well as his progress.

• In jumping training, more than anything else, variety is all-important. Going round and round over the same jump makes both horse and rider careless, and leads to dangerous situations.

• And – as usual – always acknowledge a successful jump or exercise with a pat on the back – for both horse and rider!

CHAPTER

7

PUTTING IT ALL TOGETHER

RIDING A DRESSAGE TEST OR COURSE OF JUMPS

7.1 RIDING A SIMPLE DRESSAGE TEST

The test

Ridden in a 20 x 40m arena.
Time: approximately 4 minutes.

A-X	Enter at working trot.
X	Halt. Salute. Proceed at working trot.
C	Track left.
F-M	Shallow loop, 5 metres in from the track.
C-X-A	Change the rein down the centre line.
A	Track right.
E	Medium walk.
C	Working trot.
C-A	Three-loop serpentine through the whole school, finishing on the right rein.
A	Working canter right.

A-X-A	Circle right, 20 metres diameter.
A	Working trot.
A-X	Half circle right.
X-C	Half circle left.
C	Working canter left.
C-X-C	Circle left 20 metres diameter.
C-H	Working canter.
H-K	Medium canter.
K	Working canter.
A	Working trot.
B	(In indoor arenas: on an inside track). Halt. Right turn on the forehand. Proceed in medium walk.
A	Down the centre line.
X	Halt. Salute. Leave the arena in walk on a long rein.

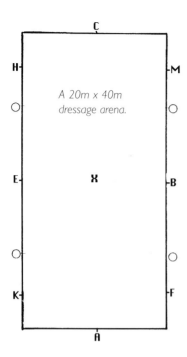

A 20m x 40m dressage arena.

C

H · · M

O O

E · X · B

O O

K · · F

A

Requirements

As well as the **corners** and the **turns** onto and off the centre line (which in this test should be ridden as a quarter of a 10-metre circle), there are **circles** and **half circles** on both reins. Also, there is a **shallow 5-metre loop** on the left rein, and a **three-loop serpentine** through the whole school on the right rein.

The most demanding **transitions** are: to the halt from working trot, to trot from halt, and from medium canter to working canter.

Lengthening is only required in canter on the left rein.

A further requirement is a **turn on the forehand** to the right.

Description

• 'Enter' means you ride in down the centre line, or onto the centre line if you are already in the arena. The judge's first impressions are based on your entry, halt and salute. It looks better if you turn early and in a wide curve onto the centre line than to ride through it and then back onto it. Once on the centre line, focus your eyes on the centre of the short side ahead of you, so that you will ride straight towards it, and not wander down the centre line. It is a good idea to increase the pace slightly, since this makes it easier to ride straight down the centre!

• 'At X Halt' means you do a downward transition to halt when your knees are level with the half markers E and B. (The same principle applies throughout the test. When something has to be done at a specified point in the arena, this always means it is done when the rider passes the marker in question.)

• You need to start preparing for the halt three to four (horse) lengths beforehand by giving subtle half-halts. By pushing the horse into the halt, with both legs equally, you ensure that the hindlegs step softly forward under the

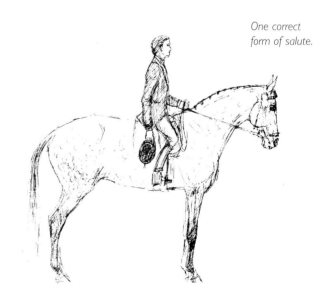

One correct form of salute.

body, and that the horse does not fall onto the forehand. If you can feel that one hindleg is trailing behind, or that the horse is resting a leg, you should act immediately the horse stops, and use your leg on the same side to encourage the horse's hind leg to take half a step forward.

• During the salute, the horse should be standing straight, on the bit, and on all four feet. If there is a mirror in the school, a glance will tell you whether your horse is standing correctly. Check your seat at the same time.

• For the salute, assuming you are a male rider, take both reins in your left hand, and grasp the peak of your hat with your right hand and take it down to your side; the hat should be held with the inside facing towards you. Women are not required to remove their hats; they should simply take both reins in the left hand, let their right arm hang down at their side, and incline their head forward slightly. Men may also salute like this if wearing a chin strap. When it is time to make the transition forward into trot, do not rush. Calmly sort out your reins and whip, if carried, but then move off as smartly as possible and without any walk steps.

• Then ride straight towards the judge in an active working trot. Remember to flex your horse to the left before starting the turn to the left onto the track, before 'tracking left'.

• The following principle applies to the whole test: if you ride the corners correctly, you will be constantly improving the horse, by suppling him and making him more 'through'. If you

have forgotten the correct technique, refer back to the section on riding turns, circles and curves in Chapter 5.

• Next, ride half way round the arena on the left rein in working trot. This gives you time to check the quality of the trot, the horse's position and your own position, and to keep the horse round, attentive and 'through' by the use of half-halts.

• On the second long side you have to ride a shallow loop, 5 metres in from the track. Always look where you want to go, in this case at a point half way between the half marker (B) and the centre point of the school (X). Keep your horse flexed to the left as you ride out of the corner and then off the track at F. One horse's length after leaving the track, change the flexion and 'feel' the horse with your new inside leg in order to obtain a right bend. During the time that the horse is bent to the right, yield your inside rein occasionally so that the horse remains light on it. One length before rejoining the outside track, change back to a left flexion and feel the horse with your left leg to begin the bend required for the corner. When riding this exercise, you must make continual adjustments to your reins.

• In changing the rein down the centre of the school, the same applies as to the entry and salute: if the impulsion is good, with the hind feet treading approximately in the prints made by the fore feet, it will be easier to ride straight down the centre line.

• Half way down the next long side, there is a transition to medium walk. Change down by means of several small half-halts, and make the transition as exactly as possible at the marker, with the hindlegs stepping softly forward under the body.

• In the medium walk which follows, the reins should be 10-20cm (4-8in.) longer, and you should accompany elastically the movement of the horse's neck. The medium walk should 'flow' and also 'cover the ground'.

• Before the transition into trot at C, shorten up your reins again, so that they are the right length for the working trot. Next comes the three-loop serpentine through the whole school. There is no easy way to determine how to make the loops the same size: each loop needs to be approximately 13 metres in diameter (13.333...m, to be exact!). The first loop touches the track about one horse's length before the quarter marker. The second loop meets the track exactly at E, and the last touches it about a length after the quarter marker.

• For each loop, establish the flexion, apply your inside leg, and repeatedly yield the inside rein. This will ensure that your horse is light in the hand and prepared for the strike-off into canter.

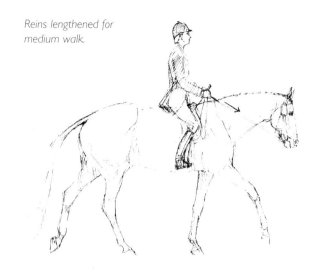

Reins lengthened for medium walk.

• Immediately before the strike-off into right canter, give a half-halt to ensure that the horse remains round and calm as he takes the first stride of canter: as you will have discovered, the first stride sets the tone for the rest of the canter! As you are performing the strike-off, you should look ahead to the next point on the circle: that is where you must go, not into the corner! Then, when you have passed through X, make the last two quarters of the circle the same size and shape as the first.

• On the circle, as you ride away from the side of the school towards X, use

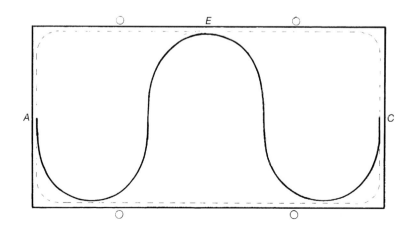

Serpentine through the whole school.

Half circle right followed by half circle left.

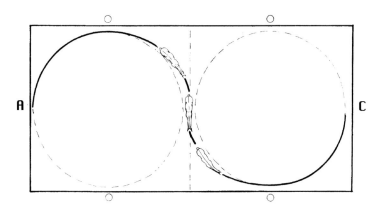

your outside rein to prevent your horse falling out onto his outside shoulder. Your outside leg should be in the appropriate position, i.e. one hand's breadth further back, to prevent the hindlegs from swinging outwards.

• Half way along the short side, at A, ride a transition to trot by means of a half-halt. If you need to use your voice to help you, do it so quietly that only your horse can hear you! Continue on the circle to X, ride straight for about one horse's length, then flex him in the new direction, to the left, and ride the next half circle.

• Ride the second half circle, on the left rein, exactly as you did the first half circle on the right rein, touching the outside track only briefly. Again, keep yielding with the inside hand, and prepare for the strike-off into canter at C by performing a half-halt. Ride the circle in working canter, finishing at C, and then ride into the next corner.

• Then comes the most difficult movement in the test, the medium canter. After riding through the corner, try to ride more forward and show a well-defined increase in the length of the canter strides. Only through

practice will you discover how much you can increase the pace, and how far before the K marker you should start to bring the horse back, by means of half-halts, to working canter. No judge or examiner who has any understanding of the training of horses and riders will expect perfection in this movement in a test of this level!

• What is important is that by the time you reach A, you have balanced the horse sufficiently, by means of half-halts, to be able to cope with the transition into working trot!

• If the test is to be ridden in an indoor school, you need to move onto the inside track for the next movement, the turn on the forehand. Just as you did for the halt at the beginning of the test, prepare to halt by giving several small half-halts. Avoid giving one big half-halt which makes the horse lurch to a sudden stop.

• When preparing to do the turn on the forehand, take your time, and wait until the horse is correctly flexed laterally and light on the inside rein, and has yielded in his mouth. It is better to pause briefly after every second step than to risk the horse anticipating the inside leg aid and throwing himself into the turn.

• Finally, half way along the short side, at A, turn right down the centre line for the salute at X. You can afford to feel a certain satisfaction at this point if you have managed to get through the test without any major blunders. The preparation has taken a lot of energy and concentration, and you can be justifiably proud of your achievement. The judges or examiners are also pleased to see a happy face at the end!

• On no account forget to praise your horse before you leave the arena on a long rein, but with a light contact.

Mentally rehearsing the dressage test

• As a preparatory exercise, go through the test a few times very precisely, and picture in your mind every detail of how you are going to ride it. At the same time, programme into yourself specific actions which you can recall or modify through verbal cues.

• Once you do something right automatically, without having to think about it, you do not need to make a conscious effort to do it, or to talk yourself through it. The more mental preparation you do, the more parts of the exercise will become automatic, and the freer your mind will be to cope with unforeseen events such as the horse shying or a different riding surface.

• Your verbal instructions to yourself, which you can work out with your instructor, are like the subtitles on a film: as you ride through the test, describe what you should be doing at specified points, and what you should

be thinking at specified points. Then develop a shortened form of this 'self talk', which should not take longer to recite than it does to ride the movement concerned.

• The test (which you will have learned by heart) should then be carefully practised with the accompanying verbal instructions. Naturally, the content will vary according to the particular problems of the horse and rider; this is your own personal set of instructions. Your cues do not need to make sense to anyone else! The following example should be seen as a basic format which you can modify and add to as required.

Example of how to talk yourself through the test

A-X Enter at working trot. X : Halt. Salute. Proceed at working trot.

(before and at A)
Turn, C marker
The line to C should run exactly through the middle of your body.

(after A)
Forwards
Active working trot.

(before and at X)
Push – light, push – light, push – light, straight
Push into a calm, non-yielding hand, after about a second lighten the aids then begin a new half-halt; halt straight.

Feel
Is the horse standing straight and square, or is a correction needed?

Left hand

During the salute, reins in the left hand, and make sure that the horse is standing quietly and on the bit.

Reins – move off

Reins in both hands again, and ride transition from halt into trot.

At C: Track left.

(after X)

Marker

Ride exactly to C.

(before C)

Flexion

Before turning, flex the horse to the left and get him light on the inside rein.

(before F – half way round the arena in working trot, left rein)

Pace, position, seat?

Check the horse's pace and position, perhaps improve with half-halts. Focus on areas of your body where faults could occur.

Flexion, bend, lighter, straight

Ride the corner correctly – this is also good preparation for the shallow loop which follows.

F-M: Shallow loop, 5 metres in from the track

(at F)

Flexion, turn, marker

Maintain the flexion as you ride out of the corner, turn when your body is level with F, then look where you intend to go, namely at the point exactly half way between B and X.

(one horse's length after F)

Reins, inside leg

Adjust the reins, and as you change over to right flexion, use your new inside leg to bend the horse right.

(one horse's length before M)

Reins, inside leg

Adjust the reins, and when you change the flexion, feel the horse with your inside leg to create the left bend.

C-X-A: Change the rein down the centre of the school. At A: Track right

Turn, marker – forwards

After turning, ride exactly to the A marker, and increase the pace slightly.

(before A)

Right flexion, inside leg

At E: Medium walk, right rein

(just before E)

Push – light, forwards

Half-halt to walk, and immediately think about riding forwards in walk.

(after E)

Reins, neck movement, active

Lengthen the reins 10-20cm (4-8in.), allow the movement of the neck, and keep the walk active.

At C: Working trot, right rein
(before C)

Reins – forward

Shorten the reins again and perform a transition to trot at the C marker.

C-A: Three-loop serpentine through the whole school, finishing on the right rein

Reins, bend, light, straight
Shorten the reins, obtain the flexion, feel the horse with the inside leg, lighten the inside aids, straighten the horse, and check that you are on course – E should mark the half-way point on the second loop.

At A: Working canter right

(before A, on the right rein)
Push – light
Half-halt before the strike-off into canter.

A-X-A: Circle right, 20 metres diameter

Outside leg, inside leg, quarter markers
For the strike-off into canter, bring the outside leg further back, press with the inside leg, yield with the inside hand, ride the circle points (A, X and arena quarter markers).

At A: Working trot
Push – light, flowing
At A, ride a transition down to working trot, forwards with impulsion.

A-X: Half circle right. X-C: Half circle left

Reins, inside leg – lighter, markers
Adjust the reins – change the flexion/bend at X, use inside leg to bend the horse, yield the inside rein, ride the circle points.

At C: Working canter left. C-X-C: Circle left, 20 metres diameter

Outside leg, inside leg, markers
Strike-off into canter as described above. Ride the circle points - C, X and quarter markers.

C-H: Working canter (go large), left rein

Corner
Ride the corner correctly after C.

H-K: Medium canter

Straight, lengthen – lengthen
Straighten the horse as you come out of the corner, and lengthen the canter strides for the medium canter.

(before the short side, working canter)

Push – light, push – light
Before the short side, bring the pace back to working canter.

At A: Working trot

Push – light, forwards
Half-halt to working trot, forwards with impulsion after the transition.

At B: Halt. Right turn on the forehand

Push – light, push – light, push – light, straight
Half-halts to obtain halt.

Right turn on the forehand.

Flexion, outside leg
Flex the horse to the right in advance, and bring your outside leg further back.

Inside – outside, inside – outside
Push with the inside leg, then use the outside rein and leg to regulate, until the turn is completed.

Proceed at medium walk. At A: Turn down the centre line

Reins, neck movement – active
Lengthen the reins by 10-20cm (4-8in.), allow the movement of the neck, and keep the walk active.

Turn, marker
The line to the C marker should run exactly through the middle of your body.

At X: Halt. Salute. Leave the arena in walk on a long rein

Marker, push – light, feel
Use a marker on the long side for reference (E or B), halt by means of a half-halt, feel if your horse is standing straight and square, or if a correction is needed.

Forwards, long rein, praise the horse!

If there were some mistakes in the test, do not get angry. You can learn much more by working out exactly why these things did not go as planned!

7.2 RIDING A SIMPLE JUMPING COURSE

Preparing to start jumping courses

Before you can start jumping courses, you must be able to jump single fences fairly reliably and proficiently.

• You must also be used to the basic canter used for jumping. The best thing is to practise this on a number of different horses. Ask your instructor if you can ride another horse sometimes – a good instructor will let you do this as a matter of course.

• Your instructor should not expect you to jump the whole course straightaway, just individual sections or sequences. Do not be afraid to tell him if he seems to be expecting too much too soon.

• In preparation for the course discussed below, you also need to have practised your feel for distances over a combination of two jumps with three canter strides between them.

• It is easier to judge the correct take-

Allow your horse to approach the jump steadily in the basic canter and give him plenty of rein in case he takes off earlier than expected.

off point if you stay a bit more upright in the jumping seat.

• If you are still not very good at judging the take-off point, simply let your horse canter up to the jump calmly in the basic canter. There are times when he needs to be able to help himself. However, it is essential that he knows how to look at the jump and balance himself. Do not interfere, and above all give him enough rein in case he jumps earlier than expected.

• If, as in the case of a jumping competition or a course you are using for training, you have access to a plan of the course beforehand, you can learn the course off by heart, during practice, so that you do not need to think about it later.

Before riding in a test or competition, you should run through the course in your mind and prepare verbal cues to help you. During your preparation you will already have discovered how best to warm up your horse. Whatever else, remember as a basic principle that it is better to do one practice jump too few than one too many!

Choosing a course

As an example of a course, we have chosen a simple jumping test which can be set up in a 20m x 40m (or larger) arena.

Requirements

The course does not require any tight turns. The first two fences are jumped from trot, and each has a placing pole in front of it. Hence, after the first fence you need to go back to trot. Both of these are cross-pole fences, and so are

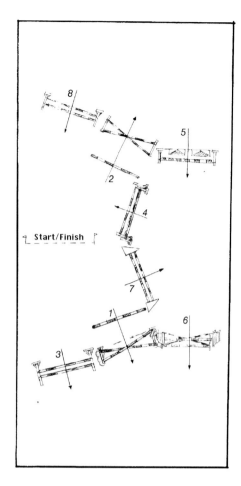

Simple jumping course, as described in the text.

easiest to jump in the centre. They should be no higher than 60cm/2ft.

The distance between each jump is equivalent to about half way around the school. The distance of three canter strides applies only to one combination of jumps (fences 5 and 6).

Description of the course

• For the salute (which is customary in some competitions) ride in trot to the appropriate point. Then circle in trot on the left rein in front of the start line until you are given the signal to start. You will have adjusted your reins, and if you have a jumping whip, you should be carrying it so that only the

Before riding in a competition run through the course in your mind.

top of the handle is showing above your hand.

• After the signal to start, ride at a brisk working trot through the start line, and then approach on a line that takes you exactly to the centre of the placing pole and the jump which follows. A few lengths before the pole, change from rising trot to the light or half seat by bringing your upper body forward slightly and transferring your weight onto your upper legs, knees and stirrups, thereby bringing it off your seat bones.

• You will know from experience and practice whether you should push the horse on or simply sit still during the approach. When you land after the first jump, bring the horse back to trot as soon as possible by using the driving aids to send him forward into a non-yielding, elastic hand (see 'half-halts').

The light or half seat.

• Once you have come back to trot, turn early enough into the second jump to be able to make an approach exactly to the centre of the jump. After the jump, continue in left canter. If your horse lands with the wrong leg leading, bring him back to trot as described above, and then strike off into the correct canter.

• Throughout the course, try to canter in a rhythm. This will also make it easier for you to learn to judge whether, to obtain a good take-off, you need to push more, or a bit less, a few strides in front of the jump.

• As a basic principle, only lengthen the canter strides when you are sure that you are going to meet the jump correctly, and then do so calmly and without losing the rhythm. Otherwise stay in the basic canter to allow the horse to compensate if he does not meet the jump quite right, for example by taking off a bit early or jumping from 'underneath' the fence.

AS A BASIC PRINCIPLE Tell yourself: Unless I can be quite sure that by lengthening the strides calmly and rhythmically I will meet the jump correctly, I will keep strictly to the basic canter.

One of the problems of this course is knowing when to turn into fences 4 and 7 in order to meet them squarely in the centre. Another problem is deciding on the length of stride between fences 5 and 6. Whether you should increase or decrease the pace in order to fit in three strides, depends on your horse's natural length of stride,

and on whether he lands long or short over fence 5.

After riding through the finish line, use gentle half-halts to make the transition down on the circle through trot to walk. Praise your horse before riding out.

On take-off, keep your upper body straight, and go forwards and downwards from the hips, with the movement.

Mental rehearsal of the course

During practice, go over the course several times in your head. Visualise it in every detail, just as if you were riding it. As with the dressage test, programme into yourself specific actions which you can recall or modify through verbal cues. What comes automatically – those things you can do right without having to think about them – no longer needs to feature in your verbal cues. This frees your mind to deal with other, unforeseeable things which cannot be planned or programmed.

When you have finished the course, whether at home or at a competition, give the horse a long rein and plenty of praise.

• When jumping a course, the time spent in the arena is much less than for a dressage test (about 70 seconds, compared with 4 minutes for the dressage test). Hence your verbal cues should also be closer together, and shorter. This also means that more of the movements must be performed automatically. This is quite feasible in jumping because many of the actions, such as sitting during the approach, the take-off, over the jump, and when landing or turning, are the same or similar for each jump.

• Discuss with your instructor precisely what you are going to say, and do – and therefore think – at specified points. The final basic format, which you would adapt to take into account the individual problems of horse and rider, might run as follows:

After the salute, on the circle in front of the start

Flexion, inside leg, lighter – listen

Keep the horse supple and 'connected' by flexing and bending him and making him light on the inside rein – listen for the signal to start.

After riding through the start

Look, centre, straight – pace

Approach squarely and to the centre of the first fence with the pole in front, regulate the pace.

After the first fence

Push – light, push – light

Push the horse into a steady, low hand, and then after about a second make all the aids lighter – then use the same technique to ride the transition down to trot.

Flexion, bend, lighter, straight

Make a point of riding the corner as a quarter circle.

After riding through the second corner on the short side, on the right rein.

Look, centre, straight – pace

Look where you want to go.

On landing after the second fence

Left, canter – forward

Left rein – check for the correct leading leg in canter, correct if necessary.

Pace?

Check you are in the basic canter, adjust if necessary.

After turning at the point you have decided on during practice, ride an approach to fence 3

Look, centre, straight – pace

After landing

Canter? – pace

Do you have the correct leading leg? Correct if necessary. Check you are in the basic canter, and adjust if necessary.

Look – turn

Look at the point where you have practised turning, turn when you get there.

After turning towards fence 4

Look, centre, straight – pace

After fence 4

Canter – pace – corners

Check correct leg and pace, ride the corners correctly before fence 5.

After fence 5

Pace, straight, centre

Go through the course in your mind exactly as you intend to ride it.

Either push or sit still – base your decision on experience, and on whether the horse lands long or short.

After fence 6

Look – turn

Look at, then turn at, the turning point.

After turning towards fence 7

Look, centre, straight – pace

After fence 7

Canter – pace – corner

Check correct leg and pace, ride through the corner correctly before fence 8.

After turning towards fence 8

Look, centre, straight – pace

After fence 8

Forward, finish, slow, praise.

8

ENTERING YOUR FIRST COMPETITION

You have now reached the point where you would like to enter a competition to obtain some outward sign of recognition of what you have learned. You want to prove to yourself and to others that you have outgrown the beginner stage.

• Before you take part in any competition, you should go through it and plan it exactly. This is the only sure way to avoid frustration and disappointment.

• You should also ascertain how much it will all cost. If you do not ride regularly (you should have been riding at least twice a week for about a year), or you do not feel confident, it may be a good idea to have a few private lessons beforehand. In addition to the cost of these extra lessons, you must allow for the entry fee, the hire of the horse (if applicable), plus possible membership and registration fees and horse transport costs.

• Also find out what you should wear.

If you do not yet own any full-length riding boots, find out if these are compulsory. You may be able to get away with jodhpur boots, for example.

• Of course, you will want to look immaculate for the competition, but do try the clothes out and 'ride them in' beforehand. Breeches or jodhpurs should be neither too tight nor too baggy; and a brand new pair of boots will only make it impossible for you to sit or apply the aids correctly! You are better off with your old, comfortable ones.

• It goes without saying that, for safety reasons, you should already own a hard hat of the appropriate standard.

BE PREPARED Tell yourself: I must be so well prepared in all the things I need to know and be able to do, that my mind is no longer taken up with them, and I can concentrate on preparing for the ride itself.

• Even if the competition is to take place in the familiar surroundings of your own riding school, the test situation itself will be unfamiliar. Here are a few tips on how to give yourself the best possible chance:

• Find out whether, before you enter the arena, quiet and seclusion are best for you, or whether you need to be surrounded by activity and distractions (see Chapter 1). Make sure that you have access to what you need.

• Are you the nervous type, who gets worked up and upset easily, so that your performance suffers? If so, make use of the appropriate relaxation exercises which you know and have practised.

• Or perhaps you are one of those people who needs an added stimulus, a bit of a 'kick in the pants', to achieve

When warming up it is better to allow yourself plenty of time for breaks and letting the horse walk.

peak performance? If so, make sure you have learned the necessary mental exercises for this too!

REMIND YOURSELF I can adjust my level of stimulation in either direction: I have learned how to 'put the brakes on' or 'accelerate' at the opportune moment.

• Also be clear in your mind as to what daily routine best suits you. Maybe you need to take your time in the morning and eat a hearty breakfast to make you feel ready and 'raring to go'? If so, you need to get up in plenty of time so that you do not end up riding on a full stomach. Or maybe, on the other hand, you are the sort of person who does best on a cup of tea or coffee and nothing else?

• Do you thrive on very little sleep, or are you no good for anything unless you get your full eight hours? Find out what works best for you, and use this knowledge to your advantage. What works for you when you are riding will also work in any other test or competition situation.

• You alone know if the weather is affecting you, or if you are having an 'off day', and how to cope with it. Do not leave anything to chance!

• For your horse, the weather and the going are factors if the test or competition is to be held in an outdoor arena. For practice, ride in the rain and on wet, heavy going sometimes, so that you are not put off by it.

• Practise your warm-up technique. Some horses take longer than others to warm up. However, always allow too much time rather than too little; it is better to keep taking breaks and letting the horse walk than to leave yourself short of time. Never do the same exercise over and over again, even if it is not working out as it should. You will only make your horse, and yourself, sick of it. Ride forward frequently in an active working pace. And do not forget to praise your horse when he has done something well in response to your aids.

• Before the test or competition, the warm-up area will probably be a seething mass of horses and riders, and it could be a case of every man for himself. Hence it is particularly important that you are well acquainted with the rules for riding in a school with other riders, especially the rules governing who has the right of way. Above all, keep your eyes open and be aware of what is going on around you, because other people can sometimes make mistakes which could endanger you and your horse.

• If you are jumping, you must have the course imprinted on your mind; you must know it by heart. In some dressage tests you are allowed a commander, or 'caller', but you should still commit the test to memory so that you do not have to rely on your reader, who may be late in calling out the instructions, or hard to understand. If you know the test, you can concentrate all your attention on riding it, and start your preparation for each movement as early as you feel necessary.

• You should know how best to memorise the exercise, and the easiest way for you to recall what you have learned. Perhaps reciting it out loud works for you, or maybe you find it better to draw it from memory on a

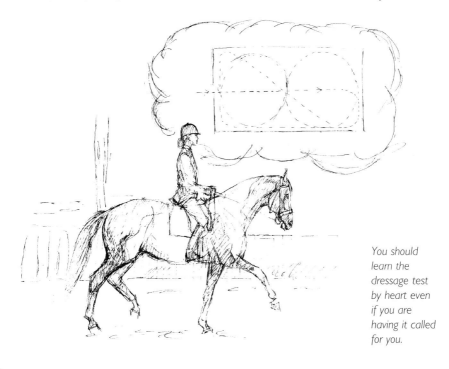

You should learn the dressage test by heart even if you are having it called for you.

piece of paper. There again, you may find it is more effective to go through it silently in your head while standing in front of the arena. Finally, a combination of all three methods may be what suits you best. Experiment, and find out what is most helpful.

• If the caller makes a mistake, by reading something out wrongly or by giving an instruction too late, this is no excuse for you to ride it incorrectly. Hence even with a caller, it is still to your advantage to know the test by heart!

• Before the actual competition, ride the course or test under test conditions, as if it were 'the real thing', without going back over or correcting anything.

• At the same time, practise putting mistakes behind you, and simply carrying on and concentrating fully on the next part as if nothing had happened. Train yourself to do this in different situations, for example not just

when you have made a mistake in the exercise, but also after your horse has shied or run away.

• Do not forget in the meantime to practise your relaxation exercises (breathing out, or simply thinking about it). Eliminating tension leaves you free to channel all your energies into the task in hand.

• When you are up against disruptive spectators, noisy children, excessively loud music, barking dogs, rustling plastic bags, and over-exuberant horses bucking and squealing around you, instead of getting annoyed, think of it as a good opportunity to further your competition training.

BE PREPARED Tell yourself: I will try to prepare in advance for all the conditions I might encounter during my test, including the worst possible scenario. Then nothing will surprise me or put me off.

Look upon distractions as an opportunity to further your competition or test training.

• Mentally rehearse the whole exercise over and over again, riding it through in your head at first in sections then as a whole. Keep an eye on the clock: in the end, the time it takes you to go through the exercise in your mind should tally with the time available to ride it.

• Talk yourself through the exercise as you are visualising it.

• Discuss your 'self talk' with your instructor, and reduce it to a series of short prompts. On no account should it take longer to say than it does to ride!

• Ask a friend to video you riding through the exercise. When you watch the film afterwards, ride with it in your mind, and try to relive the successful parts and mentally correct the faults. Even better, get your instructor or an experienced rider to go through it with you.

• If your first test or competition is due to take place at your own riding school, this usually puts you at an advantage, because you are on your home ground, and so there should be nothing to get used to or adapt to. However, the very fact that there has been a change, however small, in their supposedly familiar surroundings, is very upsetting for some horses. Experiment beforehand and see how your horse reacts, and prepare him accordingly. For example, place on the wall of the school something which would never normally be there, or ask a friend to rustle a plastic bag or wave a newspaper etc. Familiarise your horse in good time with small changes and 'disturbances'.

• If the test or competition is to take place in an unfamiliar arena, you can prepare for this by sometimes doing your training elsewhere, in different arenas.

• The ideal, of course, is to have the opportunity to practise in the arena where the test or competition is to be held. If you cannot ride there, you should at least have a look at the arena so that you can get your bearings.

• On the day, before you ride into the arena, think of a situation in which you were successful, and which will motivate you to give an equally successful performance.

GETTING IT ALL TOGETHER

Tell yourself: Whether the test is to be held at home or in a 'strange' arena, I am so well prepared and in such a positive frame of mind that I shall tackle it with confidence and self-assurance.

Before you ride into the arena, focus your mind on a previous successful experience.

At the end of all this, don't forget to say 'thank you' to your horse — he deserves his carrot, sugar lump or a bite of grass.

• Important: Do not put yourself under pressure to win. Ride to the best of your ability. You do not **have** to be placed at all costs, and you certainly do not **have** to win. Do your best, and you will be your own judge of whether you should be pleased with yourself and your horse.

• Mistakes which are your fault, and criticism from the judge, should be seen as an opportunity to further your education, and so to improve. Take a deep breath and tell yourself that even the top performers suffer frequent set-backs.

• You can afford to be pleased with yourself if you have come through your first competition with your reputation unscathed, and without any major disaster befalling you. It has been a valuable experience, and you can only benefit from it.

• Finally, do not forget to say 'thank you' to your horse for his part in the proceedings. He deserves his carrot, sugar lump or bite of grass, just as much as you deserve to be bought a drink by your friends!

Whilst it is nice to win, the main thing is that you have done your best.

FURTHER READING

Connolly, Christopher and John Syer *Sporting Body, Sporting Mind*, Simon & Schuster, 1987 (UK); Prentice-Hall, 1988 (US).

Eberspächer, Hans, *Sportspsychologie*, Heidelberg, 1987.

Foster, Judy and Kay Porter, *The Mental Athlete: Inner Training for Peak Performance*, Ballantine, 1987 (US).

Gallwey, W. Timothy, *The Inner Game of Golf*, Random House, 1981 (US).
–*The Inner Game of Tennis*, Bantam, 1984 (US).
–*Inner Skiing*, Bantam, 1991 (US).

Hölzel, Petra, Wolfgang Hölzel and Martin Plewa, *Dressage Tips and Training Solutions*, Kenilworth Press, 1995, (UK); Trafalgar Square, 1995 (US).

Orlick, Terry, *Psyching for Sport: Mental Training for Athletes*, Champaign, 1986 (UK); Human Kinetics, 1986 (US).

–*Coaches' Training Manual to Psyching for Sport*, Champaign, 1986 (UK); Human Kinetics, 1986 (US).

Rushall, Brent S., *Psyching in Sport*, Pelham Books, 1979 (UK).

Savoie, Jane, *That Winning Feeling!*, J.A. Allen, 1992 (UK); Trafalgar Square, 1992 (US).

Terry, Peter, *The Winning Mind: Fine Tune Your Mind for Superior Sports Performance*, Thorsons, 1989 (UK).

Townley, Audrey, *Natural Riding*, Crowood Press, 1990 (UK); Breakthrough, 1990 (US).

Wanless, Mary, *Ride With Your Mind*, Methuen, 1987 (UK); published as *The Natural Rider*, Trafalgar Square, 1996 (US).

INDEX

Page numbers in *italics* indicate illustrations.

Acknowledgements

Line drawings
Renate Blank

Photos
John Birt 21, 47, 57, 74, 77, 152, 156 (bottom); ExpoLife 59; Prehl 24 (both), 99 (all);
Anthony Reynolds 130; Sputz 104; from the collection of W. Hölzel 13, 31, 58, 60, 61
(both), 70 (both), 73, 79, 81 (both), 82 (all), 83 (both), 84, 109, 122, 124, 146, 147, 148,
156 (top).